SILVER AND GOLD

T0347675

Other titles in the V&A Fashion Perspectives series:

SILVER AND GOLD

by Norman Hartnell

V&A Publishing

First published by Evan Brothers Limited, 1955
This edition © V&A Publishing, 2019
V&A Publishing
Victoria and Albert Museum
South Kensington
London sw7 2RL
vam.ac.uk/publishing

Distributed in North America by Abrams,
an imprint of ABRAMS

E-book edition: 978 1 85177 981 9

Paperback edition: 978 1 85177 966 6

10 9 8 7 6 5 4 3 2 1
2023 2022 2021 2020 2019

A catalogue record for this book is available from the
British Library.

Printed and bound by CPI Group (UK) Ltd, Croydon, CR0 4YY

V&A Publishing

Supporting the world's leading
museum of art and design,
the Victoria and Albert
Museum, London

To all young artists setting
out on a career of designing

CONTENTS

PROLOGUE

Such splendour I had never seen before and may never see again. The Abbey is wearing Coronation draperies of blue brocade. Along its aisle spreads a seamless carpet of cerulean blue, changing at the Theatre's steps to a warm shade of pale honey. Clustered lights hang low at triforium level shedding a dulcet glow. The clamour of colour in dress and uniform is already here, and from my privileged seat in the Queen's Box I can see every happening and every arrival. Soon I shall be seeing the dress I have made, being worn by Her Majesty Queen Elizabeth the Second for her Crowning.

My mind goes back to the dim and uncertain days of thirty years ago when, on St George's Day, the 23rd April in 1923, I resolved to establish myself in London. In June of that year I designed my first dress for my first humble customer.

I think of those years of struggle and disappointment and I remember the three pounds a week I used to earn and how I lost that job one Christmas Eve; and I wonder irrelevantly if the number 16 omnibus still rumbles up the Edgware Road.

I think, too, of all the kindness I have known and of all the women and craftsmen who have worked to prepare the dress the Queen is now wearing.

I think of the long road behind me, leading up to this honour and bringing me to Westminster Abbey. What I suffered, learned and enjoyed on the way, is the story I presently tell.

— PART ONE —
THE PROMISE

— CHAPTER ONE —

My interest in Fashion began with a box of crayons. Because I was a sickly child, forced to remain in bed for long periods, I would sit propped up with pillows, with a drawing block against my knees, weaving crude but fantastic designs. The majority, I think, were for wallpapers, perhaps because I was in revolt against the emphatic ginger cows varnished on my night-nursery walls.

'Give the boy his crayons,' was the cry when I became tiresome.

Soon I was given a box of watercolour paints; and with it sketched my first dress design.

My cousin, Constance, saw this sketch, asked permission to have the dress made up by a local dressmaker and wore it at a Fancy Dress Ball, winning the first prize that New Year's Eve.

All my school books on mathematics, geometry and algebra, were covered with doodled designs of dresses and likenesses of the leading actresses of the day—Miss Doris Keane, Miss José Collins and Gaby Deslys. I had bought and studied so many picture post-cards that I could draw them or their dresses from memory. Easiest to draw was Doris Keane in the lovely picture frocks she wore in *Romance*. The dresses, I knew, were made in Paris. They were designed by someone called Jeanne Lanvin—a name unknown to me then but later to mean magic. So there was Miss Doris Keane swirling through algebraic symbols in rose tulle crinolines embroidered with blue butterflies, or a voluminous dress of green velvet and Brussels lace, but the majority of my sketches depicted her in a dress of swaying black velvet, white ermine jacket and cascades of limpid pearls weighted by a diamond cross.

At Mill Hill I first met Miss Kate Day, now the successful milliner of Mount Street, who has recently enjoyed the honour of making some hats for Her Majesty The Queen. At that time she was being splendidly finished off at a neighbouring academy for young ladies called Wentworth Hall. She was short, smart, plump, white and dimpled—and still is. I used to leave love notes for her in the hollow of a near-by oak tree.

One Wednesday afternoon, she encouraged my friend Edward Higham and myself to meet her and her friend, Adele Blackwood, a young Irish beauty, at a neighbouring inn called *The Green Man*, which was out of bounds, where we took tea illicitly.

Higham was a prefect; I was not. Prefects were allowed to carry a cane when walking out, but I was not. So I casually stuffed a spare cane down the leg of one of my trousers as we escaped from school, and I waved it about like Charlie Chaplin when I met Miss Day and Miss Blackwood.

On returning to school I realized I had been discovered, for the Housemaster met us on the cinder path that leads up by the playing fields. He conducted me straight away to his study.

The curly end of the cane still stuck out between the back buttons at the top of my trousers. The master removed the cane and administered punishment on the spot. Miss Day has not led me into any similar misbehaviour since.

Sir John McClure, our Headmaster, encouraged me to concentrate on my sketching and my mother, with her great feeling for beauty, was an unfailing source of inspiration; but I never felt that Father really approved of my interest in art. And yet, some years later when I found premises and decided to start a fashion house of my own, he paid my first year's rent.

Nothing could distract me from the Theatre. I was still too young to appreciate the grimness of the years between 1914 and 1918, and those years linger in my mind today as great theatre-going times, much as they must have done in the minds of countless thousands on leave from the Flanders mud. There always seemed to be dozens of delightful musical comedies that were advertised by very fine posters. One could buy albums of pictures of the actresses for a shilling.

The imprint of the Russian ballet just before the war, of Bakst and the rest of the Diaghilev school, had had great influence on illustrators' work. Perhaps the posters of the underground railways made me yearn to visit the theatres and I saved up my pocket money to pay for visits to the pit. Having willingly stood in the queue for two hours in order to secure a good cheap view, and with my chin resting on the red plush barrier that divides the back row of the stalls from the pit, I lost my heart to Gaby Deslys.

I first saw her in a musical play called *Suzette*, and was fascinated from the moment she first came on the stage, pausing only for a moment, like a humming bird aquiver with feathers and aglitter with jewels.

She was short and generously rounded at bust and hips, and her dancer's legs bulged at the calves. But the dollified pink and white colouring and her vacantly parted lips like a split plum, through which she prattled her French-flavoured English, were irresistible.

Her pencilled eyebrows were exaggeratedly arched, starting high up on her forehead, beneath a fringe and fuzz of custard blonde hair, and she had wide nostrils on a feature that possessed the prettier qualities of a small Jewish nose. Around her neck was clasped a dog collar of opals and tight strands of diamonds from which depended pear-shaped black pearls.

The play did not matter a bit, for the author had wisely based the main interest on Gaby's constant entrances in about fifteen staggering *toilettes*, designed by Reggie de Veulle.

Her succession of gorgeous dresses was quite overshadowed, however, by the even more colossal headdresses that towered, twice her height, above her. These were surmounted by fountains of aigrettes and foaming ostrich feathers, cascade upon cascade of paradise plumes, and clouds of ospreys.

Apart from her numerous lovers, who included Kings and industrial magnates, her favourite form of relaxation was roller-skating. With small steel skates clamped tight to her high-laced, grey suede boots, Mile. Deslys rolled up and down Kensington Gore, snugly wrapped up in chinchilla.

During my school holidays I glimpsed her, one memorable summer's day, arriving at Maidenhead. An enormous motor car, gleaming white, with the brass metal work of the period, pulled up outside Skindles Club. A coloured giant, smart in a tight-fitting, white cloth uniform with brass buttons, helped her to alight and relieved her of a large muff and full-length coat of white ermine. She seemed to care little for the heat of our famous English summer, for underneath she wore a dress of black velvet, fringed at the hem with white ermine tails, and her ermine hat was trimmed at either side with sprouting black and white aigrettes.

As her arched feet descended the steps of her De Dion Bouton cabriolet de ville, I noticed her remarkable stockings, partly of black silk, but mainly openworked with insertions of spiders' webs, and butterflies and roses. Going halfway up her legs, though not quite obscuring the famous stockings, were black velvet criss-crossed ribbons that came from her arched shoes, the extremely high heels closely studded with diamonds. At the vamp of her black velvet toes were two diamond *cabochons* and black pendant pearls. The well-known black pearls were around her throat which would soon be attacked by a hideous and mortal disease.

When this extraordinary vision had disappeared in the doorway of the Club, I finished sipping my ginger beer and bicycled back to Bourne End. The next day I went back to school for my last term.

In 1921, I went up to Magdalene College and fell instantly in love with the narrow streets of Cambridge, the grey colleges huddling close to one another, and behind them the velvet lawns stretching down to the quietly-flowing river. Mirrored in the still ribbon of silent water were the weeping willows that swayed like cascades of soft green feathers in the stifling breeze, and clusters of lilac and pendant wisteria bordered the verdant banks, which in the spring became carpets of close-lying bluebells.

No longer was it necessary for me to decorate schoolbooks with my artistic efforts. I was able to take watercolour painting seriously; indeed, quite early on I was fortunate to win prizes at an art exhibition. It was through this pursuit of the arts that I found my way into the Marlowe Dramatic Society which used to produce lesser-known classics, and I made my debut in a production of Swinburne's *Duke of Gardia*. From this I graduated, or descended, to the Footlights Dramatic Club, which had broader and more popular tastes. It was a club largely made up from the current polo-playing, gambling, sporting set to which I did not belong. Nearly all of them had money; I had not, but my enthusiasm made up for it. I tried to make myself useful, designing posters and programmes, scenery and dresses. I even contributed songs, both the lyrics and the melody, accompanied on the ukelele by Lord Ashley.

Jack Hulbert, who had reached the London stage from behind the Footlights, used to keep a fatherly eye on our yearly productions and brought down Cicely Courtneidge, Phyllis Monkman, Beatrice Lillie and Gertrude Lawrence. M. D. Lyon, the Somerset cricketer, was our President, and others who helped in the general decor were Eric Maschwitz, and later Cecil Beaton and Victor Stiebel.

It was a momentous day when, under the title of *The Bedder's Opera* (a 'Bedder' being the Cambridge word for a college servant), we gave a matinee performance at Daly's in London.

It was all great fun and exhilarating, but I had begun to realize that I was getting nowhere in particular. I was skipping lectures and generally neglecting important things like a career. If I wanted to become an architect I was not going the right way about it. If I wanted to become an actor, then I should have been in Gower Street at the Royal Academy of Dramatic Art. I was simply idling, and Cambridge is an ideal place to do just that.

Family matters now forced a change of focus. My mother had died a year before and my father had married again. By ill-judged investments he had lost half his fortune and, as poverty is comparative, he now imagined himself in a state of penury. He pointed out that I had inherited a little money under my mother's will.

'I don't know how long all this tomfoolery is to continue, but if you wish to spend a third year at the University you will have to pay for it yourself,' he said briskly.

But it was a woman, a complete stranger, who pointed the path which I was destined to take. The day after we had presented our musical comedy at Daly's Theatre, I drove down to Somerset, where I was staying with the family of M. D. Lyon and his brother, Beverly, the Gloucestershire cricket captain, at Doddington Park.

After dinner Mrs Lyon came over with a copy of the *Evening Standard* in her hands.

'Did you see what they say about you?' she asked me, pointing out a paragraph in a feature written by one 'Corisande'.

'Is the dress genius of the future now at Cambridge? I'd hate to presume to advise an undergraduate on his future career, but the frocks in *The Bedder's Opera* given by the Footlights Dramatic Club yesterday set me thinking as to whether Mr N. B. Hartnell wasn't contemplating conquering feminine London with original gowns.'

That was enough for me. I could hardly wait to get back to London to take up the quill pen which I then affected.

'Dear Madam' I wrote. 'Thank you so very much for the kind way in which you have written about my dress designs for the Footlights' production at Daly's. I am most interested and have decided to adopt your suggestion. Would you please tell me how I should set about it?'

'Corisande' was Miss Minnie Hogg, a leading woman journalist who was to become a great friend of mine. Her side of the story shows the strange twists of fortune's finger. On the day of the London matinée, she had gone into the *Evening Standard* office to see if there was anything of interest to report. On the news editor's desk she saw a pair of tickets and, since there was nothing better to do, decided to drop in on the show. And she had written lightly, if sincerely, about the dresses.

My pronouncement, when it arrived, shook her. However, by the very next post came a letter from a Mrs Hughes, asking to be put in touch with any young designers who wanted a trial. It was easy to arrange a meeting with Mrs Hughes, who was known as 'Madame Désirée', the Court dressmaker of Hertford Street, off Park Lane, W1.

I am not likely to forget my first meeting with her. She was an impressive lady, charming and beautiful, with a large black velvet hat set on her silvery hair and with ropes of pearls dangling to her knees.

I produced my portfolio of Cambridge designs which she fingered with satisfied nods. 'Very imaginative,' she said, 'very imaginative.'

My hopes began to soar until she offered me, not the thousand a year I rather expected, but three pounds a week. Shocked at the insult, I said I thought it would be impossible to accept her offer, but that I would let her know.

Twopence on the number 16 bus conveyed me home to discuss this disappointment with my sister. We were then living in two rather drab, big rooms in the Maida Vale district. Luckily, my sister was practical.

'Don't refuse it without careful consideration,' she said. 'Frankly, what else are you fit for? You have been to a preparatory school, a public school and a university and are still no nearer a definite career. Here is something that you can do, and do well.'

I took the job and the three pounds a week and sat down to write a heartbreaking letter to say that I would not be going up for my third year at Magdalene. Gone was the gilded youth of lordlings and young millionaires and the warm comfort of friends. Goodbye to the old grey buildings, the scented lilacs and the dreamy weeping willows. Henceforth, it was twopence on the bus or the dusty pavements of the Edgware Road, a sausage or more rarely a chop for dinner, and without a shilling to spare or an old friend in sight.

But there was little time for introspection or the mercy of self-pity. It was in the autumn of 1922 that I joined Madame Désirée.

With my box of paints I made my way up to a freezing cold garret in which had been placed a rickety table. I am not lightly depressed, but there seemed little to look forward to when my sister and I came to discuss our prospects over tea and toast at the Express Dairy in Maida Vale. Then came a new and exciting challenge. I was summoned to meet the elegant Jack Buchanan who courteously explained that he was about to produce a musical comedy with the title of *Battling Butler*, in which he would appear. He would be starring in it with pretty Phyllis Titmuss and tall, graceful Sylvia Warde, and there would be a mere two hundred costumes required. I realized that I was expected to do the entire job myself.

How I worked over those designs! I knew little about the technique of dressmaking and 'cut on the cross' meant nothing to me. Net? Tulle? Organdie? Satin? They were just names. But I did my best to find out and, night after night, sat drinking black coffee with a damp cloth around my brow until the two hundred sketches, all different in design, were completed and accepted.

My dreams of overnight fame soon faded. There was not a word about my work in the programme 'credits', but my good friend 'Corisande' gave me a tiny mention in her column which I read gratefully.

I worked as conscientiously as I could for two more months, waiting only for Friday nights, when a pay packet containing three pound notes was tactfully placed on my rickety table. It was depressing and a dead end, but at least it was a job.

Then one Friday afternoon, I was summoned to Madame Désirée's snug little room where she explained that her business no longer required a sketch artist. I need not return after the weekend.

I understood. I had been sacked. It was Christmas Eve.

— CHAPTER TWO —

My three month's experience had convinced me that I did not want to be a dressmaker. I never considered myself one, neither do I now. I am a designer and, in 1923, I wanted to be a designer of dresses for the Theatre; to be what Oliver Messel is today.

Inspired by the productions of Charles Cochran and John Murray Anderson and the charmingly-costumed revues of André Chariot, I wrote eager letters requesting interviews. From Mr Cochran I received a courteous request to call on him at his office at 49 Old Bond Street. There I went happily, having arranged my sketches so that the climax of achievement was reached in the final drawing, which maestro Cochran would see when he had duly admired the preceding ones with a growing sense of appreciation. I was ushered, however, not into Mr Cochran's room, but into that of his stage director, Mr Frank Collins.

It was nice to know later that he had a heart of gold, for on that winter morning all I could see was a lean man with a seemingly saturnine face. And he had a tongue that became bitter for me that day.

My entrance was unimpressive. I tripped slightly and caught my portfolio on the side of a chair, so that my carefully-numbered drawings slid out on to the carpet. He picked up one of my less successful works of art, naturally, and shook his head.

'This is the sort of thing we have been supplying to Delysia for years,' he said. 'It would be pointless to waste Mr Cochran's time by showing him these.'

The rest of the sketches he discarded, so I gathered them up and stuffed them back into my portfolio helter-skelter, for it did not matter now if the best came first or the first last. I left my name and address, but I did no work for Mr Cochran or Mr Chariot that year, and I was forced to conclude that the London stage could continue to flourish without my throbbing talent.

The only result from all this was that Mr Collins, a little later, recommended me to the great Gordon Selfridge. He was looking for an attractive design for smart new costumes for his famous lift attendants; famous because they were girls, something then unusual, and because they were very beautiful girls, too.

I was escorted into Mr Selfridge's office by his Social Secretary, Colonel Eric Dunstan, who was to become the celebrated 'Man with the Golden Voice' of the BBC. I had drawn about twenty pretty little pictures, which I laid out all over the desk. After a swift glance from left to right at my proffered sketches, which I still insist were extremely well drawn, even if they were more suitable for amateur waitresses in Nell Gwynne's Tea Rooms, Mr Selfridge said:

'Go away, my boy, and learn to draw.'

Later I grew to admire and like him. He would send lovely ladies to be dressed by me, and his guineas well recompensed me for that early humiliation.

The period of inactivity that followed was broken by an exciting letter, again from my good friend, Miss Minnie Hogg, saying that she had arranged for me to see 'Lucille' who was looking for a new young designer such as myself.

'Lucille' enjoyed international repute as a dress designer and dominant personality. She was temporarily installed in a small flat in Park Place, St James's, and on entering a stuffy, dimly-lit room I found this celebrated lady to be rather advanced in years. A green and silver tissue turban surmounted a wealth of bright red hair which drooped down on either side of her face, 'like a couple of fire escapes', I thought to myself. She pulled down the rather ugly lampshade of stretched green silk until it was only a few inches away from the beetroot-red chenille cloth that covered a small circular table. Then she whipped out horn lorgnettes and closely examined my dress designs under the glaring light.

'These are exactly the sort of thing I need,' she said and, in one breath, 'I trained and made Molyneux. I can train and make you. Are you free? It would mean, of course, your travelling to Paris and to New York to work with me,' she added almost apologetically.

Was I free? I did my best to conceal a surge of enthusiasm by a slightly diffident manner and hinted that I would not mind working in Paris or going to New York. Possibly I might even give further consideration to her proposal.

I walked up St James's that afternoon swinging my umbrella. Suddenly London looked very amiable and prosperous, and I was so happy that I did not even regret once more mounting the scarlet omnibus, for soon I would be flying to Paris in a silver aeroplane or aboard a gilded liner bound for New York.

'Adieu, Edgware Road!'

I waited quite a while to hear from Lucille, who had warned me that a decision would have to be reached by her on my salary. Then one morning, looking through a newspaper, I came upon one of my designs. It was illustrating Lucille's weekly piece which was called her 'Dorothy' column. 'My dear Dorothy,' she wrote, 'I've designed this lovely dress just for you.' I noticed with a start that this was an exact photographic reproduction of one of my original sketches that I had left with her a month or so earlier.

I was full of surprise and delight, for here was certain proof that I was in process of becoming designer to the great Lucille. How kind! How good!

So I wrote to her and said how glad I was that she liked my work, and when exactly did she propose that we start our business association. No answer came. I waited and wrote again; still no answer.

And then one morning I saw another sketch in print, followed by yet another, one week later. This last was reproduced on a large scale, so large indeed, that one could actually read the signature of the artist at the bottom—'N. B. Hartnell'. Since I could get no reply, I went to see a solicitor and the matter was brought into Court.

I borrowed a grey suit from my brother-in-law because I could not afford a new one myself. With me was my sister, her face half hidden in a black cloche hat and wearing a discreet black marocain dress draped to the hips *à la* Dame Clara Butt in order to assume the appearance of maturity.

My solicitor, to my dismay, suggested to the Court that I would settle for £50 and costs. Looking back now I realize that had I demanded a considerable sum of money as damages, the action might well have been a valuable precedent in a business where piracy seems to be almost a stock in trade of some of the people engaged in it. As it was, I left the courts of British justice with a promise of £50 and nothing in view for the future.

Disappointed by the outcome of my interview with the great Lucille, I wondered what to do next. There was, however, another famous dress house, that of Reville, a vast dressmaking establishment on the other side of Hanover Square, opposite Lucille's.

My faithful friend, Richard Fletcher, had recently, by good fortune, met Mr Reville and had taken the opportunity of praising me to this great man. Choosing an appropriate moment, we rang through to the House of Reville from a public telephone box in the Haymarket at about half past eleven one morning.

The telephone was one of those old-fashioned instruments where you speak into a mouthpiece like an unhealthy black lily and which, by placing the receiving end against one's ear at an oblique angle, enables two persons at one time to hear the respondent at the other end of the wire.

I listened intently while Richard talked into the mouthpiece.

'Hello. I'm a friend of Mr Reville and I wish to make an appointment for him to see the work of a young dress artist. He told me to ring him and bring Mr Hartnell to him for an interview ... Yes, I assure you it was arranged ... No, he is not a tailor. He is a young man who could be a great dress designer, like Mr Reville himself, were he given the chance ... Oh, I know Mr Reville does all his own designs, but Mr Hartnell is a most gifted artist ... Oh, thank you. Of course I will wait until he comes downstairs. I should like to explain more fully. Thank you.'

Incredible to me was the thought that the great Mr Reville himself would soon be coming downstairs to talk to us on the telephone; to talk about me. This, at last, was the moment I had waited for: to work with Mr Reville and to make Madame Lucille bitter with regret.

It became very hot in the telephone box and I started to perspire from both the heat and my acute nervousness.

'It must be a very beautiful staircase in Hanover Square down which Mr Reville is walking,' I thought, 'and it must be a very long one, too.'

Richard blew cigar smoke into the mouthpiece.

'Hello,' he said at last. 'Too busy? But he told me to bring Mr Hartnell along. Oh, he does not need any designer ... I see ... very well.'

In the Carlton Bar, Richard extinguished the stump of his now acid cigar and ordered me a brandy and soda.

We walked into the cool air of the Haymarket and entered the quiet of St Martin-in-the-Fields where we stayed for a while. As we came out Richard murmured:

'Never mind, one day you will walk out of here with a high heart.'

At that moment the prospect seemed remote. Four years later I walked down those steps again with the wedding guests at the marriage of the beautiful Daphne Vivian to young Lord Weymouth. Her dress, designed by me, was of nets of silver and gold and she was described in the Press as 'the Eighth Wonder of the World'.

Meanwhile, there was still the great house of Worth, standing with impressive dignity in the shady corner of Hanover Square, opposite Reville. But here my courage failed me. No, famous old Worth must not be bothered by unknown young Hartnell.

'I must prepare a special collection of sketches for Paquin,' I thought. 'Something truly French, but nevertheless British.'

In Maida Vale, where no birds sing and nobody seems very French or even very British, I scratched and dabbed at ten sheets of paper. Ten designs of five evening dresses (French) and five coat frocks (British).

The evening frocks did not look particularly French. They were more of Eastern Europe, goaded on by Poiret's Oriental leanings and bedizened with the jewelled titbits of Aubrey Beardsley's *Salome*. The day dresses were the very epitome of Swan and Edgar's contemporary catalogue.

To make them more acceptable, I wrote across the top of each piece of drawing paper such fulsome captions as: 'Hartnell paints for Paquin these sinuous silhouettes of sapphire satin ... Hartnell prepares for Paquin this *gamin* gaberdine gown … Hartnell persuades Paquin to create this *robe manteau* of saxe serge.'

When these were finished I placed them, each appropriately inscribed, at the top of a bundle of other of my works, tucked them under my arm and walked boldly towards Paquin's. On occasions like this I am nervous, yet defiant.

'*Bonjour M'amselle,*' I said to the completely English girl who received me at Paquin's doorway. I hazarded a guess that I might be sent to Paris to work for Paquin, and so wished to show that I had a useful smattering of the language.

I explained my errand to a mere unimportant lady and showed my sketches specially prepared for Paquin, confiding that I was quite prepared to live and work in Paris as Lucille had wished me to, but did not as yet demand an excessive salary. At the moment I was free, quite free in fact, to consider any offer she might care to make.

'You want the trade entrance,' she replied crisply, squeezing her *lorgnon* back into her black silk belt.

'I don't want the trade entrance,' I retorted heatedly. 'I am not a commercial traveller or a tradesman. I have come here to discuss the art of dressmaking. Not trade—*ART!*'

'If you have any sketches to sell, the Manager will see them. Not that we ever buy any.'

She waved her hand to the right, indicating where I would find the travellers' trade entrance. I gave one look at the first turning on the right, which is a little alleyway that still exists, running through to Dover Street.

'Art, not trade' I thought to myself. I refused to take one step down it and marched off in exactly the opposite direction.

And how wrong I was! Art as applied to dressmaking, I now realize, must be measured with the yardstick of profit and loss. The same business organization must actuate both a dress shop and a fish and chip shop. After all, the same principles apply to both; buying and selling; getting rid of stock while it is seasonable, and prompt payment.

My sister, still optimistic, volunteered to accompany me on the next job hunt. I think she realized how low my spirits were. We went to see Madame Esther, an intelligent and handsome woman with a *recherché* establishment in Grafton Street. As she still looked extremely young, my sister had assembled on the floor of our miserable flat, a very *femme du monde ensemble*. She rearranged one of my mother's still elegant hats, a cartwheel affair of black taffeta, encircled with a wide band of black osprey, and round the ankle-length hem of her black cloth coat she stitched a well-balanced hunk of black monkey fur.

Madame Esther received us with great courtesy but quickly cast my sketches aside. She seemed much more impressed by my sister's overwhelming *toilette* than by my Paquin sketches, the titles of which had all been hastily erased and re-inscribed as: 'Special designs for the Elegance of Esther.'

After a brief interchange of question and answer she offered my sister a job as 'social saleslady' (whatever that might mean) and myself a place in her stuffy little stockroom. These offers were politely refused and, with noses well up in the air, we caught the number 16 bus once again.

I gripped my Elegant Esthers whilst my sister, exuding enough dignity for the two of us, stood up in the middle of the omnibus like Queen Boadicea in the chassis of her chariot, one hand gripping the brazen brass rail and the other her disappointed picture-hat.

Some weeks later, I went to lunch with my friend Harold Warrender at his home in Holland Park. His mother, Lady Maud Warrender, quickly interested herself in my troubled state and suggested that I should see one of her dressmakers, a lady whom I shall call Miss Harper, with a view to taking a position there as a designer.

Lady Maud explained that Miss Harper, excellent business woman that she was, had need of a little financial aid and a few hundred pounds might secure me a partnership. My practical sister worked out a system whereby if I assisted Miss Harper with money she might rename her business with that of my own. The Harper could easily change to the more euphonious Hartnell.

I walked down Regent Street. Searching for the address, which was more than 'just off' Regent Street—it was very much off—I turned up one side street, then turned off up another, to find the name of 'Harper' sign-written in much-magnified feminine style of hand, above a very small shop window.

Miss Harper was a large Irish woman with a mouse-grey husband and dress. Dislike was instant and mutual. Undeterred, I elaborated my plan. For the donation of £300, which in truth was all the money I had left, she could use my name and talent for the advancement of her business. She replied that she had no proof of my talent and had never heard my name before. In both instances she was, of course, quite right. Her husband would write to me if, after discussion, they could agree to accept my small sum of money as an ordinary investment in the house of Harper.

One evening in Maida Vale the longed-for letter arrived. Although prepared to take my money, Miss Harper was not prepared to rename her business after me, since she was 'not willing to renounce the substance for the shadow.'

Some hours passed before I had the heart to show this letter to my sister whom I hated to see unhappy. Lucille, Reville, Paquin and Esther—none of them had any use for me and Miss Harper rated me merely a shadow.

I faced myself in the mirror of our lodging-house bathroom. And then the worm turned. It turned sideways and said to its sister:

'I'm going to start on my own.'

'If you do,' she answered, 'I will help you.'

It was St George's Day, April 23rd, 1923.

— CHAPTER THREE —

This book is not written as a guide to those intending to launch a great *maison de couture* in London. If anything, it is a precise warning of what not to do. No house was ever started in a more unprofessional, amateurish way. To inaugurate such an establishment now, one would have to acquire great financial backing and a number of thoroughly experienced directors. A London mansion, or even two or more mansions, would have to be found, rented or purchased, in a suitable street and reconstructed in accordance with the rules of the LCC, Westminster City Council and the Factories Act, the consideration of ancient lights not being overlooked, then decorated and carpeted sumptuously to please the expected clients.

Simultaneously one would need to engage under contract expert fitters and master tailors, with scores of accompanying workgirls, experienced saleswomen with devoted *clientèle*, furriers, embroidresses, milliners and mannequins.

In my case, the capital was £300, a box of paints and the enthusiasm of ignorance. Sooner than we dared to hope, we found in Bruton Street a sign, 'Upper Floors to Let', outside a men's tailors at number 10. It was a perfect location, being the only way through from bustling Bond Street to sedate and wealthy Berkeley Square.

We went in and were approached by a salesman. He gave me the quick up-and-down look of a good tailor.

'I don't want a suit,' I said. 'Could I look at the upper part of the house?'

'For commercial purposes?'

'I'm a dressmaker,' I said.

'What firm, sir?'

'Er—Norman Hartnell's,' I told him.

'I'll fetch Mr Bradley, sir.'

Mr Bradley, the tenant of number 10, turned out to be a benign gentleman who looked surprised at being confronted by such young people. He stroked a dubious chin.

'How big a staff have you?' he asked.

'About … about twenty,' I plunged.

'That may be too large for the size of the premises,' he commented, leading us upstairs.

This former Georgian dwelling had the usual L-shaped first floor: in effect two rooms, the smaller one at the back. Above were two more floors, of diminishing size, and without the lush parquet of the first.

'This is wonderful!' I exclaimed. 'Just what we want. But we won't need all three floors.'

'That is a pity,' said Mr Bradley, 'because I am letting them in their entirety. The rent is £850. Exclusive,' he added thoughtfully.

'Oh, very,' I agreed. 'It's a very exclusive neighbourhood.'

'Exclusive of rates,' corrected Mr Bradley. 'By the way, have you two young people anyone—*responsible*—acting for you in this matter?'

In response to a telegram my father came hurriedly to London, lunched with the helpful Mr Bradley at the Savoy and paid the first year's rent in advance.

'Try and make this last for twelve months. It is not a case of if you go broke, it is when,' he said grimly.

My sister had volunteered to oversee everything and I imposed upon the poor girl the combined duties of manageress, receptionist, saleswoman, bookkeeper and stenographer. Her office was a table and a chair behind a grey velvet screen, which kept falling over, revealing her in all her capacities.

I remembered, too, that at Madame Désirée's there was a nice middle-aged English woman dress-fitter. She usually wore a moleskin coat, had moles on her face, and, believe it or not, her name was Madame Mole. She was fortunately disengaged and lived at Muswell Hill, where several neighbours were her clients, some of whom she later brought to us. She agreed to join the staff, though actually there was no staff for her to join.

With difficulty we managed to engage a few young ladies for the workroom. Miss Holliday, Mrs Leach, Miss Griffin, Violet Durling,

Mabel Cox and little Nellie Todd. The last-named was only half a girl, because according to the rules about the cubic capacity of workrooms only six and a half ladies could be accommodated in ours, and little Nellie was the seventh. Thus only half of her was permitted in the workroom. *In toto* she was against the law!

Whenever the painstaking inspectress entered the building, we bundled Nellie off.

'Nellie, your hat and coat quickly. Go and buy sandwiches.'

'But I've just been and got you a dozen, Miss,' argued the wide-eyed little girl.

'Never mind, Nellie, don't argue. Mr Hartnell is a hungry man. He needs lots of sandwiches. Now, go along and get some more.'

Once, when there was no time to send her out, Nellie was told to go and sit in the showroom and look like a customer.

'How do I do that, Miss?'

'Oh,' said my sister, 'just sit back in a rather careless manner and yawn a little.'

'I don't mind doing that, Miss, but I'm not going to buy nothing,' she said firmly.

'No, Nellie, dear, of course we don't expect you to do that, but you will make people think that we are busy. Here's my fur coat, Nellie, and for heaven's sake powder your nose!'

'But I haven't got a puff, Miss,' answered Nellie. My sister instantly applied a cloud of *Quelques Fleurs,* but even this did not make her look very much like a customer, I fear.

One dull afternoon Nellie rushed up to me, white with fright and powder, and said:

'Honest, I think I've just seen Gladys Cooper.' And so she had.

By mistake the lovely Gladys Cooper had walked into our showroom, seeking the second floor in which she intended to install her business of Gladys Cooper Beauty Preparations. Before I could reach her, she had walked sedately upstairs, carrying a long and elegant walking stick of the kind then made fashionable by Reville. She was just withdrawing her patronage from Reville and giving it into the inspired hands of Edward Molyneux in Paris. Her tenancy of course helped with the rent but, seeing that dreamlike vision floating upstairs every day, I longed hopelessly to make a dress for her.

Incidentally, Gladys Cooper was the first woman of whom I heard it said that she had subjected herself to a diet in order to keep slim. Her self-imposed torture was of milk and potatoes only, for two days a week. At that time the average woman never thought of dieting. In fact the usual practice was for clients having a fitting to arrange it for one o'clock, which would take them through the luncheon hour and save them from the temptation of a rich meal. Meanwhile, they could vent their ill-humour, caused by hunger, on my unfortunate staff.

One of my important roles was that of 'matching boy', and perhaps this needs a little explanation. There is a wonderful race of women, mostly small girls, who haunt the West End every day in search of correct materials, of the right shade and texture, for the big dress-makers. These are the 'matchers', a tough breed, depending for their livelihood on the shrewdness and accuracy of their matching. While Madame Mole and her girls sat in my room, cutting out and sewing, I joined the queues of jostling matchers at Peter Robinson, Bourne & Hollingsworth and John Lewis—at least, there always seemed to be queues when I was in search of five yards of beige lace at 5s. 11d. a yard.

Not knowing the protocol of the matching world, I would wander up to the head of the queue.

'Here, what are you doing?—and who do you think you are?' a little Cockney would ask.

'Oh, I'm Hartnell,' I would say with a sickly smile.

'Never heard of you. Anyhow, get to the back of the queue and wait your turn. Go on, do the bird's trick and hop it!'

I decided that the matching queue was not my particular milieu and one day my sister engaged a busy little body called Louie. Having devoted her quick wits to my business ever since then, she is now my head stock-keeper, and a well-known figure in the West End world of dressmaking.

Relieved of my matching duties, I found more time to make colourful sketches of quite unwearable dresses. My sister would look over my shoulder.

'Norman, dear, I know that a band of magenta coq feathers stitched across the stomach of an apple-green satin dress is most original, but wouldn't a simple little dress of black wool or brown tweed, or even a grey flannel suit, be … nice?'

'No, it would not! I despise simplicity. It is the negation of all that is beautiful,' I said haughtily.

My father had recently called to acquaint himself of our rapid progress towards bankruptcy. I complained of claustrophobia which could only be cured if I had rooms of my own in, say, St James's.

He reached for his hat and gloves.

'My boy, it is better to live over your business than over your income.'

An unhappy addition to my small staff was an elderly stock-keeper whom I shall call Miss Blank. Because the stockroom was so far away, she was able to rule without proper supervision. She quickly gained my confidence and persuaded me that it would be much better to pay cash regularly to all the travellers and earn for myself a spotless reputation for prompt payment.

To bring about this splendid state of affairs it would be more businesslike, she urged, if I supplied her with cheques made payable to 'self' or 'cash' and signed by me. I blush to admit that I did so. And one Friday Miss Blank did not return from luncheon.

On the Monday morning I sauntered across the glass gangway and down the iron steps that led to the stockroom, to find my sister at bay, surrounded by a crowd of angry travellers and tradesmen demanding money for accounts which had been unpaid for several months. Apparently, they had been rung by Miss Blank on that Friday afternoon and told that my firm was nearly bankrupt.

I was now many hundreds of pounds in debt, and disaster was imminent. We begged for the grace of time to effect payment, and a few last remaining War Bonds were sold, leaving us almost penniless. I wrote pitiable letters, explaining my unfortunate plight to all those nice women clients whose bills were as yet unpaid. In some instances their dresses were not even finished or delivered. They responded magnificently and I shall always be grateful. Also, to dear Gladys Cooper who volunteered a cheque for another quarter's rent, unnecessarily in advance.

In penitence to my sister and, soundly ashamed of myself, I drew lots of little black dresses and numerous flannel suits.

Soon after that an unexpected visitor arrived. She was a handsome capable Irishwoman with white hair, blue eyes and a characterful nose.

'I am Miss Doherty,' she announced briskly. 'I have just left Molyneux in Paris. You, they tell me, are the new genius. I made Molyneux. I can make you.'

The last time I had heard these words spoken was by Lucille. In spite of these two clever women I reserved the thought that Molyneux might have made himself!

'I can see I am going to be very useful to you,' she continued.

'But I am not looking for any more staff,' I explained quickly. 'Furthermore, I could not possibly afford anyone as important as you.'

She raised a protesting hand.

'I would not dream of accepting any salary, *as yet*' she affirmed. 'That may come later. I will be with you on Monday morning next. Goodbye until then.'

My sister and I greeted her as she arrived promptly at 9.30am. The two women were frigid towards each other.

'Now, when can I meet your directors?' she asked.

'You can't, because we haven't any! You had better see us. We are partners, you see.'

'How splendid,' she beamed, conscious of no opposition. 'You, Mr Hartnell, I shall call S.P.'

'What the hell for?' I asked, nettled.

'For Senior Partner—S.P.—you see? And you, Miss Hartnell, I shall call Martha.'

'My name is Phyllis,' said my sister.

'Never mind that. You're Martha to me, my dear. Where are the fitting rooms?'

'There is one behind the screen.'

'Where is the office?'

'Behind the other screen.'

'Where is the stockroom?'

'Over the roof and down the stairs.'

'Who is your stockkeeper?'

'She's gone.'

'Splendid! Then you, Martha, go down there at once, out of the way. I will take over your desk. I want two chairs. One for myself and one for you, S.P. You must always sit beside me. Have you any books, S.P.?'

'Yes, at home—Dumas, Dickens, G. A. Henty.'

'No, no,' she cried. 'I mean business books. Your order books, stock books, invoices, docket system. *Tour books*.'

'We haven't any.'

'Then, Martha, get some. Who is your fitter?'

'Madame Mole is.'

'Fetch her to me.'

Poor Madame Mole was promptly packed off with a week's salary.

'We must have a French fitter. Have you the *Morning Post*? Look, S.P. Here is the very thing! "A young Frenchwoman in London seeks employment as *première* in first-class dressmakers"—address in Tottenham Court Road. Martha, here is five shillings. Get into a taxi and bring her to me at once.'

So was engaged Madame Germaine Davide, the famous 'Mam'selle' who started with me at £4 a week and soon rose to a salary of £2,000 a year. Before her retirement she enjoyed the honour of making the wedding dress of Her Royal Highness Princess Elizabeth, now Her Majesty the Queen.

I was despondent and apprehensive that financial disaster was always just around the corner. Furthermore, I was hurt and disappointed that the famous and well-dressed women of England had not yet bothered to come and see my work. Even Madame Mole's sedate and faithful *clientele* were slipping back to the suburbs and away from me.

Richard Fletcher called to see me in my blackest mood of depression. He made a crisp prophecy.

'Norman,' he said, 'you have been dressing Muswell Hill. I will bring you Mayfair!'

He went on to propose that I give a show to the Press. I stared back in frank amazement. Up to that time I had never even given a Dress Show, even less had I heard of a Press Show. I left all the arrangements to Richard and Miss Hogg while I got on with designing the dresses.

I was left alone all that winter to continue, untroubled, building up my collection, with the intention of holding my first show some time in March of 1924. My sister and I had long since come to appreciate the charming efficiency that lay concealed behind Miss Doherty's brisk manner. In the workroom she acted as interpreter between my university French and Mam'selle's Berlitz School English. Helped by these two meticulous women, who judged the value of my proffered sketches and advised on style and cut respectively, my work took on a new aspect. I was beginning to understand how much lay between the designing of a dress, which gave me intense pleasure, and its transformation into something that women would buy.

Of necessity I began to learn more about the cost of materials and their distinctive qualities; and I observed at close quarters the incredibly complicated process of measuring, cutting and repeated fitting which is the essential prelude to the completed construction of just one dress.

About a week before my exhibition of dresses a director of a large London drapery business called upon me. At the time of the Miss Blank crisis he had been the only one who did not press for immediate payment. On the contrary, he had assured me that his firm not only condoned my outstanding account but solicited my continued custom. He hoped, moreover, that we would purchase all our requirements from his firm, to the exclusion of others.

I had been overjoyed by this generous suggestion and accordingly bought almost my entire supply of materials from this one accommodating source.

He now came to the point quickly.

'My directors would like the account settled—in full.'

I stared at him in dismay.

'But I can't! Not all of it. Surely, you understand? Not all at once.'

He handed me a cigarette. 'I am afraid those are my instructions. If you find it impossible to pay, we will have no alternative but to take over your business. We can allow you ten days to render payment.'

The steel teeth of the trap were about to snap down on my helpless neck. Ten days! Ten days! In a week my show was to take place. I dare not tell Miss Doherty or even my friends, Miss Hogg or Richard Fletcher. Instead, I wrote to my father in the South of France.

It was a long time before he received my letter, since he was moving along the coast from Nice to Monte Carlo and beyond. I doubt if any designer has ever worked under such mental stress as I did during those ten days of doubt, threat and suspense. From nine in the morning until seven or eight at night I stood by the side of Mam'selle, watching my designs materialize beneath her gifted fingers and grow gradually into life on my lovely mannequins.

In some schizophrenic way I managed to split and freeze the one half of my mind that was in the grip of financial terror and apply the active half to the creative effort of producing the intended forty-seven models. Excitement ran high as little black dresses for the day vied with peacock-jewelled glory for the evening. Golf suits, flannel suits and coat frocks lay on hangers side by side with tea gowns of pink satin and pearls or lilac lace. A foaming feather band of shaded blue-grey was stitched on to the hem of periwinkle blue velvet, rose ostrich fronds to pale pink lace and one outrageous garment of crimson was emblazoned with a gilt thread dragon. The colour beige was everywhere—in wool, georgette, marocain and *guipure*. Silver tissues were hung with cascades of crystal fringe that fell from a girdle of diamonds and sapphires. Some were frightful, some beautiful.

There were two outstanding dresses that completed the collection. One was the model wedding dress of silver tissue, veiled in white tulle and weighted with garlands of silver and gold lilies, which was bought by the Hon. Daphne Vivian of brunette beauty for her wedding to the young Viscount Weymouth at St Martin-in-the-Fields.

The other was also of silver tissue, clouded with white net and scattered with silver flowers, which we copied for beautiful Lady Lettice Lygon. Afterwards Lady Lettice told me that, wearing this dress, she had attended a party at a home for crippled children. As she drifted from room to room the children were enthralled with this ethereal vision. They caressed the drifts of snowy tulle and fingered the silver lilies. A little girl begged to be given one of the flowers. Lady Lettice plucked one off her dress and gave it to the child; and then, as she moved from bed to bed, each request for a lily was granted until Lady Lettice found, with tears in her eyes, that no lilies were left gleaming on her gown.

Meanwhile, my sister, supported by Miss Doherty, arranged the showroom furnishings. The usual rows of uncomfortable little gilt chairs were hired and faced a square, stepped platform of grey velvet, with screens and draperies of more grey velvet which were to be pulled aside by a little coloured boy dressed in the habit of the popular Nubian figures, then featured in the *décor* of nearly every smart apartment. Long-stemmed lilacs towered in every corner.

The stage was set … but still no letter from the far-off Riviera. Two or three times a day my sister and I would run to greet the postman at the top of the stairs, but the stamp of France was never on our letters.

The guests started to arrive and Miss Sidonie Goossens, kindly supplying the music, started to pluck her harp strings. Now the harp is perhaps the loveliest instrument of all, but a piercing arpeggio on it for a mannequin wearing 'No. 1—First Tee', a golf suit, is not the most appropriate accompaniment.

During the display I sheltered behind the tall, grey screens that swayed ominously, and the platform squeaked as my faithful mannequins stepped from side to side in the confined space. Above this sound I heard the murmur of criticism, the chatter of women and the ceaseless clatter of teacups.

Before the show I had refused to move from the sanctuary of my hiding place. I could not summon courage to meet the few women journalists or the assembled audience.

When it was over at last, I still refused to move from my sanctuary into the showroom, but my sister expressed the view that it was exceedingly bad manners not to greet the great ladies who had graced my first exhibition. I agreed reluctantly.

I met the Countess of Kimberley, nursing a funny little schipperke on her knee, the beautiful Viscountess Massereene and

Ferrard, lovely Lady Lavery, and the unforgettable Lady Oxford and Asquith—taut and slender—dressed in grey and the colour of cigarette ash all over. Her intelligent face in profile was a piece of fine fretwork. She spoke in a deep mellow voice.

'My dear young man, you've had a beautiful day and your future should be beautiful too. The golden ball is at your feet—now kick it!'

I promised to kick it as hard as I could.

As I escorted her to the door the postman was running up the staircase to deliver the afternoon mail. The ash from one of her everlasting cigarettes dropped on to her grey glove as Lady Oxford shook my hand.

Then she was gone and I was holding a letter with a French postmark. Inside the foreign envelope was a small letter of admonishment, together with a little slip of banker's pink paper. It was my reprieve.

The following day was the third anniversary of my mother's death and I decided to go down to a quiet churchyard in Sussex and visit her grave. I went downstairs into the salon, redolent of yesterday's show. Cigarettes, perfume, hot clothes. I pulled out some lilac from the flower vases, put them under my arm and walked through the early morning London streets to Victoria Station.

Very much later in the day, over a cup of coffee, I suddenly glanced up at a man opposite me and my eye caught the newspaper in his hand. It couldn't be missed—my own name was staring me in the face! Hurriedly, I bought all the papers and this time read them through. There was a great deal about young Norman Hartnell, and a complete report of the Dress Display. With mingled pride and apprehension, I read my first press report. I had become a newspaper story almost overnight. After the first flush of notices there were others, with headlines like 'From Magdalene to Mayfair', and a great deal of play on the words 'light' and 'blue'. What astonished me as much as anything was that I was so suddenly and incredibly *accepted*, as if I were part of the Mayfair scene.

Within a week I was unwittingly (but quite willingly) plunged into a controversy with Cardinal Logue, who had said that 'The dress, or rather the want of dress, of women of the present day is a crying scandal.' Lady Oxford told the *Daily Express* that in her opinion 'women's fashions have never been prettier or more sensible than now'. Dame Sybil Thorndike declared that 'women's dresses are far more decent than they have been for ages'. But Mr Norman Hartnell had other views. 'I think there is not a good word to be said for the short-skirt fashion. Skirts have never been worn so abbreviated in the whole history of dress. Ankle-length dresses are delightfully graceful but they certainly should not be shorter.' My show fascinated the old *Daily Graphic* to the extent of a whole column about Dolores, Epstein's model, who wore some of my specially statuesque dresses.

I only wish I could say that Mayfair was thrilled by this new arrival in its midst and that my salon was packed with eager clients. Not so, for although I won many friends, I was not French, and my designs had not come all the way from Paris.

Mam'selle summed up the situation: 'Every English lady wishes something that is French. If it were not for the pure beauty of your dresses you would not sell a single one.'

A woman would see my collection, choose a dress, approve of the material, the colour and the price; have her measurements taken, and fix an appointment for a fitting. Then a casual question: 'By the way, whose model is it?'

'Mine,' I would reply proudly.

'Oh, is it not a Patou or a Lelong? Not a French model? Then, I think I will reconsider it. No, on reflection I won't take it, thank you. Good afternoon.'

I suffered from the unforgivable disadvantage of being English in England.

There was only one thing to be done; to acquire a Parisian cachet, however spurious. I knew that the leading buyers from America flocked to Paris every February and August (nowadays it is January and July) in search of the new styles. They were the accredited arbiters who could set seal or doom upon a designer. With youthful bravado, I decided I must show my collection that August of 1927 in competition with the great couturiers of France. It was a flashy but brave little gesture actuated by complete ignorance of what lay before me.

In a spirit of blissful optimism, I flew to Paris, the city of eternal enchantment, to make arrangements for my first show ... and I landed up to my neck in trouble.

— CHAPTER FOUR —

In Paris I decided that the newly-opened Plaza-Athénée was the right *mise en scène* for me. The director, Monsieur Armbruster, was most helpful. He advised me to engage a small reception room leading off the hotel's flowered central courtyard. He volunteered to undertake all arrangements for seating accommodation, lights, chairs, refreshments, etc.

Back in London, I assembled my new collection of dresses and visited the French Consul's office to inquire what formalities might be required. I was told that there were no restrictions whatsoever. It appeared that Paris would welcome me with open arms.

One day in August, hot and breathless, my boxes, my dresses, my mannequins and I sailed across the Channel and eventually found ourselves in front of the customs authorities at the station.

The first question was ominous.

'Where is your *patente*?'

This, it seemed, was a formal document which entitled a foreigner to the privilege of temporary trading in France. It was impossible to extricate my dresses from bond unless I possessed one.

The official shrugged away my protests. He advised me to return to London, apply to the French Consul and await the grant of my *patente*, and until then it was useless to return to France.

Within twenty-four hours my collection was due to be shown to the international Press, and the dresses were in the tight grip of the French *douane*. I went to the Hotel Ritz, feeling like a rowboat without a rudder. By happy chance, I was introduced to the Hon. Evan Morgan, the future Lord Tredegar. He listened sympathetically to my story.

'I think I may be able to help you,' he said smoothly. 'My cousin is the British Minister here, Sir Eric Phipps.' An appointment was made for me to call upon His Excellency the following morning at eleven o'clock.

When I found myself outside the impressive entrance of the British Embassy, it needed some courage to continue alone, unaccustomed as I was to great buildings and distinguished diplomats. I was led through a series of fine rooms to the Minister's study.

Sir Eric Phipps turned out to be a most engaging and delightful man; neat and dapper, he was dressed in the smartest of striped trousers, with elegantly-buttoned boots of fawn cloth and gleaming patent leather. In his observant eye was secured a frightening monocle, through which he regarded me sternly across his desk.

Firstly, he reprimanded me for my lax conduct in not obtaining the correct credentials, but when I had passed the responsibility to the French Consulate in London, he relented. His masterly manner indicated that rescuing helpless dressmakers from such predicaments was a perfectly normal part of his duties. I sat quite still, feeling as though I were back at school. Sir Eric picked up the telephone from his desk, made a few mysterious calls and then dictated a letter.

Half an hour later, I returned to the customs. They had apparently received a telephone call which had not left them in the most amiable of tempers. Our trunks were opened out on the damp, dirty floor, which looked as if a herd of cattle had been the last passengers through the customs. Out poured Miss Muffet, Little Pickle, Highland Lass, Lac des Cygnes, Goosey Gander, Forty Winks, Grandma's Garnets, and the rest of our precious models. There was nothing we could do to stop them, and in the end we simply carried the dresses in our arms to the waiting taxis.

The dresses were hurried round, one by one, to the hotel and whisked on to my two models, Eileen, a brunette, and Shirley, a blonde. These two admirable young women carried on their shoulders the weight of the entire collection of ninety five dresses.

The Press turned up in force, mainly from curiosity to see this daring young Englishman who was bringing fashion to the very home of fashion. They wrote most generously, I must admit, and I felt that this publicity alone made the venture worthwhile. 'His picture dresses are delightful in their characterization of youth and feminine loveliness …' said a kindly critic. One unusual fashion note was observed. Each dress had a little lead medal on a piece of string somewhere about it—the *plomb* of the customs.

There were very few buyers present, but the one who did buy launched me very satisfactorily on the American market. This was a famous New York connoisseur of dress, Mr Herman Patrick Tappe, who chose, I recall, the two extremities of the collection, a Scottish tweed suit called 'Country Cousin' and a copy of the silver and gold wedding dress I had made for the Viscountess Weymouth.

Another man also helped to make that afternoon memorable for me. He was Mr Bocher, then directing the all-powerful *Vogue* magazine in Paris. He came up to me afterwards and said:

'You know, young man, your model 'Goosey Gander' is the best black lace dress in Paris.'

I must explain why I felt this to be the finest compliment that could be paid me. It is hard to invest a black lace dress with any quality of novelty. Here is the criterion by which women unconsciously judge a designer's true skill.

'If you will dine with me tonight at Larue's, I will tell you a few more things,' he said quietly.

Across the dinner table that night Mr Bocher gave me his views on art and life, on dress and sales, on fabrics and passing fashion, on his own career. He came from the State of Maine and his Christian name was Main, yet nothing he said made a greater impact on me than his summing-up of my first show in Paris. 'I have never seen so many incredibly beautiful dresses so incredibly badly made.'

The world now knows that kindly and experienced man as the *couturier*—Mainbocher.

I waited one more day in Paris, but no other buyers came to see me at the Plaza-Athenee. Back into the trunks went the London dresses, only two of which had been shipped to New York. The hissing train steamed out of the station and I thought of Dick Whittington, sitting dispirited on an uncomfortable milestone as he heard the bells ring out from the great city he had just quitted. And I said to myself, I said: 'I'll jolly well come back here again!'

I did, and surprising results followed the announcement of my second attempt to storm this Bastille.

'*M. Norman Hartnell, de Londres, montre sa collection à Paris dans un ancien hôtel de la rue St Honoré, ayant appartenu à la Marquise de Pompadour, et maintenant Magasin d'Antiquités …*'

Firstly, the words 'Magasin d'Antiquités' should be remarked upon. It was a measure of the dislike an Englishman could incur in bringing English clothes to the French capital of fashion. Previously, I had given my showing in a suite at the Plaza-Athénée. Now I could not find a suitable hotel. Happily, I had a very good friend in Paris, a rich and sophisticated woman called Miss Alice Archibald, now Lady Clark Minor, for she married Clark Minor, head of the British War Relief in the United States.

She acted as my liaison and tried desperately hard to find a suitable suite of rooms for me, but in spite of her neutral social standing she could persuade no hotel to open its doors. Paris to me was a closed shop. It was a shop, however, an American antique shop in the Rue St Honore, that eventually agreed to house me.

Miss Archibald, exasperated by refusals from every hotel she approached on my behalf, had cleverly hit on the idea of asking an American friend, Miss Dezengremel, to allow me to show my dresses in her interesting apartment, once occupied by Madame la Marquise de Pompadour, against an original background of quaint antiquities.

There was one most frightening disadvantage. On my first visit it had been lack of a patente to trade that had brought me up against the French laws. This time it was some clause in the lease—I believe connected with insurance—that insisted that someone should sleep in the shop every night in order to guard the dresses. Therefore, I had to make my own bed there, or rather, make use of an ugly and uncomfortable Empire bed that was part of the stock of antiques. This would have been bad enough, had I not been surrounded by a collection of devil-masks of African witch doctors.

Waking up suddenly in the deep of the night, disturbed by the noise of a rusty sword falling across the snout of a leering gargoyle, I found myself in this Chamber of Horrors that looked all the more weird in the dismal light that filtered from an Oriental lamp.

I was frightened out of my wits. 'To the devil with dress designing,' I muttered. 'I want to get out of here and go home.'

With the morning sun came the most golden, glorious and rewarding success that any designer of dress could desire. Through the door of Madame de Pompadour's salon thronged an excited crowd of men and women representing every great buyer from the United States of America, Canada and elsewhere. They praised and applauded me and, more important, they stayed to purchase. Dollars poured into my lap.

The splendid London model girls, who worked with the guts of British carthorses, even turned themselves into temporary sales-women to cope with the flood of orders that overwhelmed us.

The American buyers went out into the streets, generously and loudly extolling my work and literally dragging in their professional rivals to see the show. Many of them returned, and they bought and bought and bought. With no time to halt for food and drink, we worked and sold until late into that exciting night.

The French *concierge* from below demanded from us that we shut the apartment down. But with a few of our francs in her palm she herself shut up. We scribbled the orders and cabled them home. When it was over, some of my girls lay flat on the floor, utterly exhausted. Miss Archibald called in a very smart hat and took us all out to supper.

Not all our visitors were so charming. One arrived next morning, a beautiful creature who offered herself for work. She explained that she had had much previous experience with the great 'Madame Rivoli' in the nearby Rue de Rivoli (I have invented both name and address).

After my success, news of which had spread through Paris the previous day, I welcomed her and allotted her many of the best dresses, much to the chagrin of my own English girls.

Instead of going out for the luncheon hour, she stayed in the models' room, having brought with her her own repast which, in France, is somewhat unusual. She lingered and fingered the dresses in a knowing way, asking the source of the materials. She worked for that one day but did not return for her money. I do not suppose she had much need of that money, for on the morrow she was back in the Rue de Rivoli, working as usual as the highest-paid and permanent mannequin for the world-renowned, yet inquisitive, 'Madame Rivoli'.

But these were mere irritations in that exciting atmosphere of triumph. I shall not quote everything from the spate of eulogy that poured from the Press. 'Norman Hartnell's collection is as adorably witty as a Ronald Firbank novel' said one scribe. Another was kind enough to say that I had 'deflapped the flapper' and had become 'the debutante's very own designer'. Practically the whole of the article on Paris fashions in a leading New York paper was devoted to my dresses.

But the most valuable summing-up of this visit did not come until many months later. It was made by the Baron de Meyer in the influential *Harper's Bazaar*.

'Paris dressmakers cannot claim the new long dresses as their own innovation,' he wrote. 'Long dresses were brought in by young Mr Norman Hartnell from England last year.'

— CHAPTER FIVE —

By the spring of 1934, eleven long years had slipped by. They were years of progress in my business not unmixed with the alternating periods of exaltation and depression which are inevitable in a profession like mine. The well-dressed women of society had flocked to my dress parades and had bought generously, and the Press was proving both amiable and encouraging.

But not until 1934 had I started to make any considerable financial profit. Everything had been ploughed back into the business. Larger accommodation became imperative and once again I reviewed the Mayfair scene. There was one perfect house almost opposite me, number 26, but it seemed too large and the rent was far too high. Yet it was perfectly constructed for a *maison de couture*. Only the ballroom floor and the front bedrooms on three floors were still in their original state, but the back part of the building was already transformed into strictly modern workrooms, conforming to the Factories Act. My sister and I worked out a plan, to arrange the vast back room as a *cabine des mannequins*, a retiring room for the *vendeuses*, a powder room for the clients, a telephonists' room, packing room and ten fitting rooms. I longed to occupy the place, imposing, practical and capacious, but resisted the temptation. We left with a sigh to find out which way the West End wind was blowing.

The answer was emphatic. The wind was blowing westward. I wanted very much to move as far west as Belgravia which to my mind was, and still is, a far more desirable district than Mayfair. But Belgrave Square did not care for trade winds, neither did Berkeley Square, although it cherished Gunter's Teashop, then the only shop in it.

Sunderland House was offered me. It was an island site most admirable for the parking of cars, but built of much marble and too overpowering to convert into a dress house. I also scorned Grosvenor

Street, where the rents were a third of Bruton Street. Mrs Somerset Maugham advised me shrewdly to move into Portland Place, perhaps the grandest thoroughfare in London, and to take an Adam-built mansion there. But I feared that my clients might not care to take their limousines northwards across the hubbub of Oxford Street.

Months passed and my bank balance continued to blossom. Irresistibly I found myself again inspecting the premises at 26 Bruton Street. This time I did not hesitate; a decision which was perhaps guided by a little professional jealousy. Victor Stiebel had opened his chic salon at the far end of Bruton Street, where he was selling clothes rather like mine, only more cheaply. Also, Edward Molyneux of Paris had opened his elegant pale grey showroom in number 36 Grosvenor Street, where he sold dresses not at all like mine and much more expensively. Quite frankly, I could with pleasure, at that time, have packed Victor and Edward into a wheelbarrow and tipped them both over Beachy Head.

My sister and I sat down to think about decorating this lovely Georgian house, which was once the home of the Hereford family. I got hold of several decorators' pots of paint. The body colour was white, into which I tipped Hooker's green, meridian green, a touch of gamboge and a mid-grey. This mixture produced a subtle tone of green resembling lichen, celadon green or that elusive shade that gleams on the back of the leaves of the silver willow when softly stirred by the breeze. I dubbed it Hartnell green. When a firm of contractors delivered a lorry load containing 600 gallons of green paint the colour of a faded bicycle shed, I promptly returned the lot. The right creamy tone finally arrived. When displayed in great areas on the staircase and on the showroom walls, it seemed as one of nature's natural backgrounds to every colour of flower or rainbow. It did not impede or detract from the roughness of home-spun tweeds or the silver and gold of bridal gowns.

Pale green Swedish marble and dark green Italian marble were used for the entrance hall, and vast expanses of carpet stretched across the floors in the same tone. Velvet was specially dyed in Paris for the long curtains and upholstery, and great columns of faceted mirrored glass supported the high ceilings. I bought about a dozen magnificent coruscating chandeliers, some of which were original Regency pieces, while others were made up of Waterford crystal. They now blaze aloft, as the only compliment to the beauty of the antique in an otherwise modern salon.

All this was costing me a great deal more money than I had anticipated. I despaired at the cost of it and once even wanted to telephone the landlord in the middle of the night to stop it all. I had nightmares of toppling crystal columns and chandeliers crashing into a chaos of marble and carpet.

There was, of course, no turning back. I set to and produced a luxurious and expensive collection. Everything now hinged upon the success of my presentation which was fixed for one evening in early September, 1935. The ladies and gentlemen of the Press turned up with the intention, I felt, of good-natured support. But after the third mannequin had tripped across my luxurious green carpet the lights went out all over the house. I walked out on the lead roof and began chain-smoking. When I finally returned to my laughing guests, they congratulated me on a clever publicity idea in switching off the lights.

The rest of the collection was shown by candlelight, carried in the hands of the giggling mannequins. They looked pretty in the glow of the flickering flames, which pleased the men, while gifts of flowers and scent mollified the lady journalists, who had been relieved of reporting the show since there was nothing they could see to report upon. Although everybody else enjoyed the evening, it was not a very happy one for me.

My fortunes had improved since that fateful second visit to Paris and, as a dress designer, my style had changed very considerably. I had begun as a designer for debutantes and soon developed into the ultra-sophisticated designer, sometimes for women who were dangerously too chic. The third period began to take shape in the 'thirties. And each of these periods of transition brought new problems and new personalities.

The influence of the stage was a strong factor in my development and I had tried to forget my unhappy experience with *Battling Butler*. I had longed, since my Cambridge days, to design both the costumes and *decor* for a great stage production, imagining that one would have a free hand. In this I was, of course, proved quite wrong. Very often the scenic designer has first choice and usually takes the best colours for use throughout his set of scenes. The upholsterer and the artificial flower-makers then stake their claims. So does the lighting expert, who usually floods the stage with dreary marmalade-coloured amber lights, taking the guts out of everything, including the stage set, the dresses, and the leading lady's face, causing much embarrassment for everyone else concerned. With what money and from what colours are left for her limited option, the leading lady has to choose her dresses.

The dressmaker, in collaboration with the actress, evolves charming designs and the sketches are submitted to the producer, with estimates. The business managers of both dress house and theatrical office then wrangle for several days over the price. The author of the play may then disapprove of the suggested dresses because the heroine's character has to be sympathetic, and these dresses, he considers, are too smart.

This actually happened when Basil Dean gave me beautiful Frances Doble to dress for Noël Coward's play *Sirocco*. For her big love scene I was told to make a blue serge skirt with a beige silk blouse, and for the heroine's visit to a local fiesta, to recapture the failing passion of her errant lover, a kind of schoolgirl's gymnasium dress in wish-wash blue satin.

In the heat of the love struggle, she had to roll about on the floor with the hero, Mr Ivor Novello, and her navy blue haunches became covered with the grit and dust of the dirty, stage floor. It all ended in the ridicule of laughter and the drama of disaster.

The fascinating Yvonne Arnaud asked me to make a set of grand dresses for her part in *The Improper Duchess*. They turned out to be very beautiful and she looked most regal in them. But on the final fitting of her *negligée*, a two-piece affair of jade green velvet over a gossamer shift of pale green chiffon and lace, I was told that a cushion of a sharp, apple-green taffeta had pride of place on the sofa upon which Miss Arnaud was to recline with her stage lover.

'Why not change the cushion?' I suggested. This was completely ignored because the author and producer had meanwhile become attached to this acid-looking cushion and I was told to remake, within two days, another elaborate *negligée* but this time in tones of cherry and pink.

At the first dress rehearsal, the hideous cushion was quickly discarded to make way for Mr Hartley Power, whose manly frame, together with Miss Arnaud, now monopolized the sofa.

The play ran for years.

I was fortunate enough to have my work noticed by the great Cochran. He was a most delightful and considerate person to work for, and commissioned me many times to supply dresses for his magnificent spectacles. For one scene in a Coward revue I designed and made about twenty bathing dresses for a beach scene in the South of France. Frankly, they were frightful looking things, made in the wrong style of fishnet, fish scales and fringes of bobbing corks. They were much more appropriate as fancy dress for a marine fantasy than for twenty of Mr Cochran's chic young ladies supposedly bathing on the beach at Cannes. At the fateful moment of the 'dress passing' on the stage of the Pavilion Theatre, the critical but kindly Noël found himself compelled to refuse the entire bunch. Naturally, I felt disappointed but he was perfectly right.

A few days later, the lovely Lily Elsie opened in Ivor Novello's play *The Truth Game*. I can frankly claim that the dresses I made for her were perfect and that I left the theatre delighted. Next morning I received the following telegram. 'Hearty congratulations on your superbly beautiful dresses for Lily Elsie last night—Noël.'

There is a sequel to this. A woman buyer from a famous New York store said that she was entrusted with the selection of beach clothes for a new branch, to be opened in Miami. 'Did I know who in London made such things?'

I unloaded the dresses that I had made for the theatre. She was delighted, for what was unsuitable for the stage was excitingly wearable on the beach in everyday holiday life.

My saleswoman asked far more than I should have received from the theatre management. It was one of the few occasions when a mistake ended in profit.

In dressing artistes of the music hall and cinema it is sometimes difficult to over-estimate the value of vulgarity. When I gulped hot chocolate with Mistinguett in her Piccadilly hotel boudoir, and sipped weak tea with Mae West at the Savoy, I found that both these glamorous women were intelligent and charming, but I realized how much of their great fame and fortune they owed to an excess of sequins and dazzle.

It was Mistinguett, the outstanding star of the Paris music hall, who, in spite of her French sense of economy, ordered from me a dress similar to one which she had seen worn by the exquisite Evelyn Laye in *Give me a Ring* at the London Hippodrome. It was a thick meshed dress aglitter with sea blue sparkles, weighted with silver fox. A most expensive garment.

My work for the stage has also brought me many valued friendships which have sometimes been severely tested. Evelyn Laye and her husband, Frank Lawton, are two very good friends. So are the brilliant Bebe Daniels and her amiable husband, Ben Lyon. But this friendship was greatly strained when, at the Variety Artists Ball held at the Albert Hall, the crowds parted to give way to Miss Daniels making a sensational entrance in her Hartnell gown of lemon yellow, embroidered with diamonds and gilded pearls. A moment later Miss Laye was announced, making her sensational entrance in her Hartnell gown of lemon yellow, embroidered with diamonds and gilded pearls. And Evelyn Laye's place was at the very same table as Bebe Daniels.

The crowds of theatrical worshippers watched for the imminent clash between the great ladies of the stage. But, conscious of the situation and of their public, these two clever actresses curtsied to one another with a set-fair smile, embraced with fervent kisses, linked arms, cracked a bottle of champagne and, with professional perfection of poise, faced a battery of clicking cameras.

The safety valve for my lack of dressmaker's diplomacy was in the fact that both these women had auras of equal quality. Had one been more beautiful than the other, the fat would have been truly in the fire. But the jet black brunette beauty of Bebe Daniels was equal to the ivory white, blonde beauty of Evelyn Laye, and fortunately for me they happened to be the best of friends.

I need not have worried so much, for my morning mail contained two telegrams. One said, 'I hate you and I hate Evelyn Laye. Close my account at once. Signed Bebe Daniels.'

The other said, 'I hate you and I hate Bebe Daniels. Close my account at once. Signed Evelyn Laye.'

But I get on quite amiably with their husbands who still sign their wives' bills.

There was one occasion when my much-loved opulent gowns, designed for a big musical called *Home and Beauty*, taught me an expensive lesson. It was brilliantly written by Sir Alan Herbert and lavishly produced by Sir Charles Cochran. The leading lady was the Viennese singing star Gitta Alpar and other ladies were Miss Binnie Hale, Miss Iris March and Miss Sepha Treble.

Now Miss Alpar had a will of her own and hair as red as fire. On the question of costumes she was a trifle difficult. Worried about putting on unwelcome weight, she had undergone an operation which had left scars on various parts of her anatomy. She wore high cut necklines and tall Russian boots. Her dresses, of course, were ground length and chin high.

'I wish fur for my neck,' stated Miss Alpar.

'I would like fur as well,' agreed Miss Hale.

'I like fur, too,' murmured Miss March.

'So do I,' echoed Miss Treble, and all the ladies looked appealingly at Sir Charles and myself.

We melted. And the various ladies were pelted thus—Miss Alpar had red fox, Miss Hale had black fox, Miss March had white fox and Miss Treble had silver fox.

'I would like muffs,' added Miss Alpar. So magnificent fur muffs were added to each lady's already rather extravagant *ensemble*.

'In my hats I want paradises,' thought Miss Alpar. So, too, thought the Misses Hale, March and Treble.

'Let these pretty ladies have what they want, Norman,' sighed Sir Charles.

So Miss Alpar wore orange paradises, Miss Hale wore peach pink paradises, Miss March wore white paradises and Miss Treble wore black paradises.

'I would wish my orange dress to have many, many sequins,' observed Miss Alpar.

The Misses Hale, March and Treble observed that they, too, would wish sequins. So Miss Alpar had copper sequins, Miss Hale had gold sequins, Miss March had silver sequins and Miss Treble had black sequins.

The first night arrangement favoured Miss Alpar and seconded Miss Hale, while Miss March and Miss Treble hovered on either side looking extremely pretty. The music was lilting and lovely, the scenes magnificent, the costumes attractive and everybody acted and sang as though their hearts would burst. But the audience disliked the whole affair and it closed after a short run.

My sole reward was the pleasure that I enjoyed in making all these staggering dresses for these lovely ladies.

In spite of a few disappointments in some theatrical ventures, I must admit that the dressing of the stage gave me tremendous pleasure and many memories. I remember a Jewel Ball at Claridge's and draping the gorgeous Gladys Cooper in ivory *panne* velvet and pearls as the White Pearl Bride; Gertie Lawrence in gunmetal velvet and silver fox as Black Pearls; Jose Collins in white satin banded with black astrakhan; Lily Elsie in wisteria mauve; Frances Doble in white chiffon and Benita Hume in brown chiffon. More recently I remember Vivien Leigh in ink blue tulle, and the contemporary beauty, Margaret Leighton, in gold beaded chiffon collared and cuffed in glossy mink; a Chinese suit for Linda Christian, and gigantic dresses for Eileen Joyce, trailing half-way across the concert platform. Margaret Lockwood in floating white muslin, Anna Neagle festooned with lilac. I sent a bevy of mannequins to Claridge's to give a dress display for Marlene Dietrich, the most beautiful of all. She viewed my dresses from the edge of her marble bath.

I remember Norma Shearer, sweet and quiet, sitting up in bed at the Dorchester, eating porridge and treacle while I showed her clothes to take back to Hollywood. In the next room her husband, Irving Thalberg, was ceremoniously selecting ties from Hawes and Curtis.

I have designed for most of the leading actresses of the past two decades. Gertrude Lawrence was to me the most irresistible and fascinating woman of them all. She was not a beauty. Her nose tipped up into the air and her Adam's apple, as big as a pickled onion, wobbled up and down in her throat as she talked or sang.

Her speaking voice had a petulant and plummy note and her singing voice was always off-key. The flatter she sang, the flatter one fell for its fascination, and if she were ever on-key, which was rare, it was a disappointment. Her hair fell naturally across a somewhat bulbous brow, and, at that time, was neither crimped by hairdressers' tongs nor bleached into any other colour but that mid-brown which so gently became her.

She moved with ineffable grace and her manner of walking across a room has never been excelled by any other woman, either on or off the stage. Her lissom body was a perfect clothes prop for any *couturier*. I believe there is a modern phrase to express admiration of a smart woman: 'My dear, she could tie a towel round her and look divine!' This Gertie actually did. In one play in which I dressed her, there was a small scene in which she entered the stage from an imaginary bathroom literally tying a towel round her, and she looked more alluring in that beautifully tied towel than in any of her dresses by Molyneux or Hartnell.

I first noticed Gertrude Lawrence singing a pert little song in one of Chariot's revues. It was called 'Winnie the Window Cleaner'. She wore a hideous overall of common butcher blue cotton. Instead of jewellery, her properties were a mop and a slop pail. No *ensemble* could have been less becoming but she tied that crackling apron round her slender thighs as none of Jacques Fath's *premières* ever thought of doing during that 'apron' period.

I clearly remember the first luncheon I enjoyed with her on a very warm, spring day at her apartment in Portland Place. The hall was in apple green and olive green. She showed me her bedroom, which was a lovely mixture of ivy leaf velvet with Chinese wallpaper of green leaves and pink water lilies and pink flamingoes. A little room like a cigar box was panelled with pine and plastered with photographs of every star of the theatre and film world, and with one or two even more illustrious names.

Each room smelled of a different scent. The pine room was thick with *Cuir de Russie*, the dining-room was heavy with Chanel's *Numero Cinq* and Worth's *Dans La Nuit* perfumed the bedroom. Gertie explained that she resprayed the rooms daily and, fetching a *vaporisateur* from a handy little cupboard, she exuded a lovely odour all over the cushions and the backs of the sofas. Suddenly sinking to the floor, she sprayed large expanses of the carpet around the fireplace and over by the door with this very expensive essence.

Wiping her damp fingers on a long jade green chiffon handkerchief, she concocted an overpowering cocktail. I started to sweat a little as we sat down to lunch. The decoration of the dining-room also undermined me somewhat. It was, I think, of pale grey enlivened with flower vases full of dyed green tulips, but the large windows were surprisingly curtained in gathered luxury of solid silver sequins.

Now, as some people know, I am more than partial to the jolly glitter of sequins, but yards and yards of these pretty little objects massed together like a coat of mail and coruscating in the midday sunlight of Portland Place (whilst I still felt hot and queasy from the scented cocktail) were not a soothing accompaniment to the eating of bloaters and mustard sauce, her favourite dish at that time.

Yet the most embarrassing object of modern art in Gertie's dining-room was the dining table. It was a thick sheet of clear glass. Through its pure clarity I could see Gertie's elegant feet in emerald leather, one slender ankle crossed neatly over the other. Unfortunately for me, I could also see my own feet and they looked awkward and stupidly pigeon-toed. I shuffled them around a bit, arriving at a stance of a quarter to three, which looked worse. With an assumed nonchalance, I flung one foot over the other, as Gertie was doing, but the effect was not quite the same.

I leant my wrist on the sharp edge of this hateful glass table, compressing some nerve or other, so that a blob of bloater at the end of the chic fork started to waggle. Adding further to my nervous distress

I could see, too, that my knees were now trembling. In an effort to hide my nervousness from the unruffled Gertie, I spread out a white table napkin across my knees, but being well-starched, shiny and slippery, the thing fell to the floor. I stooped to the carpet and, upon straightening myself, cracked my head against this invisible table.

'Darling, whom do you consider the best-dressed actress on the stage?' said Gertie, the tactful creature, trying to make me forget my embarrassment and leading me into a conversational rut which she knew that I knew.

My answer should have been 'you', but I missed my cue.

I thought it wise, anyhow, to give the palm to someone Gertie liked and, searching in my mind for any other actress against whom she nurtured no implacable jealousy, I said:

'Beatrice Lillie.'

'Bea Lillie!' echoed Gertie. 'But Beatrice isn't a woman, she's a clown.'

'Isabel Jeans is lovely,' I added quickly.

'No, darling, not Isabel! She's divine, dressed up as Nell Gwynne, or as a Regency strumpet, or a model girl in *Chu Chin Chow*, but not for the modern dressing of the stage today, dear. No, *not* Isabel.'

'Well, what do you think about Gladys Cooper?' I questioned.

'What do I think about Gladys? Gladys is a true beauty, darling, but only a beautiful statue. She would be divine as Venus de Milo with lots of drapery all over her and no arms for some unfortunate director to tell her how to use. To me, darling, Gladys is just a flag-pole, a lovely, tall, divine, beautiful flagpole!'

It seemed safer now to turn towards a previous generation. So I muttered: 'Well, there is always Marie Tempest.'

'Good heavens!' shouted Gertie, 'there always has been and there always will be Marie Tempest. No young actress can ever get near the London stage today because there is always Marie Tempest. Darling, what on earth can you admire about her clothes ?'

'Sort of neat,' I ventured.

'Neat! That sofa's neat, but it's just upholstered, like she is.'

'Well, Gertie, she does make lovely entrances, swinging a picture hat,' I protested.

'And have you ever seen her wear one, ever put one near her head? All that hair and one of those terrible hats! And those tricks—in a woman her age! Darling, you're mad! Try again.'

I was no longer equal to this struggle. Furthermore, I was starting to feel very sick. My knees felt like two oscillating jellyfish. Bloater bones had tickled my throat and a cloying smell of Chanel still lingered on my fingers. The sequined curtains glittered and dazzled. It was too much; sequins, Chanel and bloaters. Hurrying from the room, I arrived just in time at the end of the passage.

Gertie was extraordinarily sweet. She brought me black coffee whilst I lay on the spinach-green velvet bed, surrounded by unwelcome pink flamingoes which, so pretty an hour ago, now seemed to resemble Mr de Valera and Nellie Wallace. She seemed to have forgiven me and forgotten all about Bea the clown, Gladys Cooper's arms, Isabel Jean's shortcomings and Marie Tempest's picture hats.

I kissed her goodbye.

'Of course, Gertie, you know quite well that you are the best-dressed woman I have ever seen,' I murmured.

'Well, darling, why couldn't you have said so in the first place!'

I last saw Gertrude Lawrence on the stage in that lovely New York production of *The King and I*, in which she created the leading part of Anna. I went round to her dressing room and we drank cool beer together.

Perhaps it was a hint of her approaching doom that made her look extremely tired, or it might have been the demands of the long leading lady part. She asked countless questions about England and expressed her longing to come back to London to see the Coronation of the young Queen.

It was my last night in New York, and with promises to meet we bade farewell. I never saw her again. Since her death I have thought of her constantly for there was no one like her and there never will be.

The word 'Glamour' has become so vulgarized by over use that it has become the small change of advertising currency. But in the sense in which I understand the term, Alice Delysia has had the aura of glamour for me since, as a schoolboy, sitting in a box at the London

Pavilion, she had sung to me. She seemed then the very essence of the naughtiness which existed for me in some kind of adolescent fairy tale. I did not dream that one day I should know her well and fall head over heels in love with her.

Our first meeting happened in rather a dreary way. It was in a small fitting room. I had been visiting New York and while there received a long cable from one of my *vendeuses*, Miss Paula Knight, saying that Alice Delysia wished me to make her dresses for a new play called *A Pair of Trousers*. She had hitherto always been dressed by Jean Patou of Paris.

I rushed off to Madison Avenue to buy a sketch block and a box of paints, and hurried back to my rooms at the Waldorf Astoria where I drew a variety of designs which were accepted. I got back to London in time to be present at the first fittings, pulled the little curtains aside and officially met Alice Delysia. She wore high silk stockings and a hat with tall feathers sprouting out like black fireworks. It dared to ask her out to lunch at Quaglino's, where she told me that she was going on a short holiday to Marrakech before the play. She asked me to go with her, an exciting invitation I promptly accepted. A day or two later I convinced myself it was wiser to send a telegram saying I was suffering from a slight cold and did not feel sufficiently fit to go to Morocco.

After the first night of the play in which she appeared with Miss Violet Vanbrugh, the critics were not very warm. Her clothes, however, were mentioned several times and one dramatic critic gave prominence to her sweeping evening coat of amber velvet, trimmed with red fox fur. The dress she wore underneath was a tight-fitting sheath of amber, gold and tortoiseshell crystals. Her jewels were of amethysts and diamonds, and with all this she wore a gigantic bunch of parma violets. A quiet *ensemble*, I suppose, for Delysia.

By now I was on the most amiable terms with the delightful Alice and one Saturday night I called at her dressing room to drive her and a few of my friends down for a long weekend to my small house in the depths of Windsor Forest.

I had recently had one of the guest bedrooms decorated in tones of blue. Soft Wedgwood blue and white chintz curtains and periwinkle draperies were held up by a flight of white cherubs hovering over a bed of sapphire blue velvet. The carpet was of navy blue and the soft lighting came from orchid pink candle shades. The chandelier lamps and wall brackets were of original Wedgwood ware.

I discovered that Delysia was quite a different person away from the footlights. She would be up early in the mornings, walking round the lake. She would sunbathe behind a tree on the lawn and the moment it started to rain was the moment she chose to go for a long walk. She would wear a raincoat, wipe all vestige of make-up from her face, and tie a handkerchief round her head.

In return she invited me to stay with her and some other mutual friends at her villa on the Plateau de Bidart, which was situated high on the cliff and gazed out over the Bay of Biscay.

The place was prim and neat and, in her own house, Delysia seemed much more of the *femme de ménage* than the *femme du monde*. We would bathe a great deal of the day and at other times she would busy herself around the house dusting and polishing, with a scarf round her head. The food was of the simplest but she was a superb cook, making perfect omelettes. A bottle of *vin du pays*, several fruits, cheeses and good coffee was the usual menu. Then she would wash my clothes and darn my socks.

'Ah, dear,' she would philosophize, with her head bent over a length of beige darning wool, 'You may count your real friends on the fingers of one hand and find you have fingers to spare.'

But she would disappear at about five o'clock to freshen up for the evening. This process took up to two and a half hours. My duty was to play barman and produce supplies of 'White Ladies', her favourite cocktail.

At about half past seven a slight cough from the top of the stairs would warn us to be conscious of Madame's presence and she would float downstairs, the perfected Parisienne, in a clinging gown of black or white, her hair coiffured as though Antoine himself occupied the adjoining room.

The face that all day had gleamed with oil and perspiration was now superbly made up; dreamy eyes, luscious lips in a background of soft caramel skin, and against the warm brown flesh glittered diamonds that fell like icicles from her ears to her collar bones.

We interchanged these holidays at Ascot and Biarritz for a long time. Then came the news that Cochran was to present her in a big production called *Mother of Pearl*, and I was to do the dresses. The story, rewritten by A. P. Herbert, was an amorous tale of a mature woman whose natural daughter from an old romance unwittingly falls in love with her mother's own young lover. It was a great part for Delysia who wore a magnificent *negligee* of pink tulle and pearls, a black velvet crinoline stuck with diamonds and, I admit, a jolly little green velvet suit by Victor Stiebel!

Her great entrance was made in front of a gigantic turquoise blue satin curtain, wearing the first solid sequin dress I had ever made. It was a skin-tight affair of sapphire blue with glittering cape to match. Delysia wore no undergarment nor did she need holding up or holding in. Nature had given her the perfect silhouette.

One night at the Café de Paris, Florence Desmond came up to us and said casually: 'Hello, my dears, I hear you two are engaged.'

'Yes,' said Alice. 'Isn't it wonderful?'

I agreed it was wonderful. The next evening the papers announced our engagement, and soon the house was in a state of uproar, for she immediately drove down to Ascot.

It was a trying evening. We were besieged by reporters and photographers but were finally able to discuss the matter calmly and coolly. It was prudent that she should return right away to the Savoy. As her car swept out of the drive, my life changed back again. Next day, by mutual consent, we inserted notices in the papers to say there was no truth in the announcement.

As Delysia once said to me, 'You love for a little while in your life, but when that love is over, then the things you have loved for a little while together will keep you for always together.'

She is now married to a handsome and most delightful Frenchman and is extremely happy. She is still beautiful and to me she will always be beautiful.

— CHAPTER SIX —

It should not be inferred that in the gay, carefree early 'thirties I designed exclusively for the stage. The fashionable matrons and their daughters, some dazzling and others with ambitions to be so, came in gratifying numbers to my salon.

Mayfair was still a village of great houses, and although many were doomed to physical destruction, their hostesses were putting up a brave rearguard fight in defence of the old social values.

Everything revolved around the Courts in summer, the presentation of debutante daughters, nieces and cousins; with at least one big dance between May and July, at the end of which the houses were theoretically empty, the owners being on their way north to the moors, via Goodwood and Cowes.

Their presiding deities were the dowagers, who had vivid memories of how things were done in the opulent, colourful reign of Edward VII, but tinged with memories of the dignity and manners associated with his august mother.

I had the very firm feeling that we were about to see the doom of the flappers with their short skirts and Eton crops, and I was proved to be right. Eton crops were to go the way of all fashions, and before long I was to cause quite a sensation by daring to employ a model girl whose hair was actually unshingled.

Not that all the young beauties of the day wore their hair short, or smoked their cigarettes out of ridiculously long holders. The influence of the great country houses was still strong. Evelyn Waugh, in that glorious satire of the twenties, *Vile Bodies*, draws an absurdly vivid picture of a debutante dressed in the traditional English fashion. 'Lady Ursula wore a frock such as only Duchesses can obtain for their elder daughters, a garment curiously puckered up and puffed up and enriched with old lace in improbable places, from which her pale beauty emerged as though from a clumsily tied parcel. Neither powder, rouge nor lipstick had played any part in her toilet and her colourless hair was worn long and bound across her forehead in a broad fillet.'

Yet, on the other hand, there was the international set, the Embassy people, the extremely smart women who went to Paris for their clothes, the personalities whom Michael Arlen limned so cleverly, and who stood rather aside from the great county families.

Perhaps the most outstanding beauty of all debutantes was Miss Margaret Whigham, now the Duchess of Argyll. Her perfection of appearance recalls the pink and white of camellias, and her hesitant stutter adds one more charm to this beautiful person who showed the women of her age how to use cosmetics, how to dress, how to be a success, and how to behave whilst becoming one.

Her contemporary rival, both in beauty and fame, was Lady Bridgett Poulett. Her cameo features were topped by the highest of brows and the most pointed of widow peaks. Her oval face was moulded by two lines of contour that ran contiguously each side of her face, forming another perfect oval at the point of her chin.

There were many other beautiful clients, too lengthy to list. Some were only distinguished for their eccentricities and vagaries of behaviour. When I hear the expression 'feeling blue' my mind's eye travels back to one morning long ago when my receptionist called me on the internal telephone.

'There is a lady downstairs,' she announced, 'who wishes to see you. She says you do not know her, but she knows you as a blue, and would like to discuss the matter with you.'

In those early days I was exceedingly shy and very frightened of meeting strange people, but at the same time most anxious to gain new customers.

'I do not think I have had the pleasure ...' I began.

'But now you have,' she interrupted with a giggle.

Unclasping her locked fingers, crammed into blue kid gloves, she patted the sofa. 'Do sit here.' I sat there.

Fumbling in a large bag of crude blue, she brought out a matchbox of even cruder blue enamel, encrusted with the diamond initial, 'D'.

'Now we have the pleasure, the mutual pleasure, of meeting—shall I say out of the blue?' she said.

'Oh, how delightfully expressed,' I answered bravely.

'But we shall be friends, shall we not, Mr Hartnell? For our bond is blue, is it not?'

Whereupon she once more opened her handbag and showed me a recent press-cutting concerning the number of blue model dresses I had shown in my current collection.

'There,' she cried. 'That proves it! I have read all about you. I feel I know all about you, but I did want to hear all about yourself from yourself. Now tell me, what do you feel about blues?'

I was slightly at a loss. Did she wish me to express my opinion of the outstanding Oxford and Cambridge athletes, known as 'Blues'? Did she perchance think that I harboured some schoolboy hero-worship of the Royal Horse Guards, the 'Blues'? Or was I addicted to the slow-time American music called 'the blues'?

'I am very fond of blues in every way,' I assured her.

'I know it!' She breathed heavily. 'Look at me. Don't you see blue everywhere?'

Somebody must have told her that blue suited her. Certainly she had blue eyes, but then nearly every Englishwoman thinks that she has been blessed with blue eyes, when they are really grey, green or slate-coloured. This lady was blue from top to toe. A portion of blue felt was folded like a carpet slipper on her head and held in place by a crescent of blue cotton cornflowers. Her dress was of larkspur voile, a summery affair, revealing sturdy kneecaps which protruded between the pendant points of the voile. Cuban-heeled shoes which were, I hazarded, originally of grey lizard's skin were now stained with a smeared blue dye.

She leaned towards me anxiously, awaiting my opinion.

'Yes,' I said, 'it's all awfully pretty.'

'Ah, I knew, I knew,' she repeated. 'Our love of blue will bind us together. Life is always blue. It's blue by day and blue by night. My home is called 'Blue Lagoon'. My husband, the Commander, was blue—the Navy, you know. He was drowned and the sea was blue.'

'Oh, how sad,' I said, quite sincerely, for her watery blue eyes looked a little sad although, of course, I realized that she was somewhat too troubled to remain normal. I was sympathetic and somehow liked her.

'No, I am not sad, just blue, you know.' And she whipped out a fine little handkerchief embroidered with the initial 'D' in blue.

'The "D" stands for Delphine. I was originally christened Daisy, but I call myself Delphine, short for Delphinium, you see. I feel happier that way. I always wear blue, you know, and I wish you would design me some lovely blue frocks to wear in my house. Evening gowns and tea gowns of blue chiffon, kind of floaty stuff, to wear with my sapphires.

'You would love my house. That's all blue, too. Blue brocade and blue chintzes which are patterned in blue delphinium. Everything tones with the carpet which is a deep sort of blue. You would love it. Perhaps you would come and stay with me some time.'

I thanked her for her very kind invitation, but imagined the whole thing might become a little too blue for me.

Yet another wonderful client with a colour problem was the Duchess who called to order a copy of a dress similar to one I had made for Gertrude Lawrence. She was a famous hostess, renowned for her beauty, her wealth, her great houses and her unerring taste in all things.

The lovely Gertie was appearing at that time in a play called *Can the Leopard?* in which she swooped and swooned, floated around and flirted with Kim Peacock, her leading man. The dress she wore whilst doing all this, when shimmering under stage lighting and moulded to her lovely lines that made her seem some fluttering goldfish, was a trailing affair of scarlet chiffon. The Duchess wanted one like it.

I gathered together every shade of red chiffon I could find and showed them one by one to the Duchess, who proved very hard to please. The fitting room seemed stuffy with all these fiery tones. Becoming impatient, I tried to hurry her decision.

'Why net this one?' I cried, waving about trails of geranium chiffon. 'Geranium is a jolly shade and most becoming.'

'It is not at all becoming,' she said sharply, 'Geranium is a colour that is a challenge to my face, which I do not appreciate.'

The Duchess had a truly beautiful face, but it was rather pallid.

'Oh, well, why not pillarbox? It lights up so well at night.'

'It lights up most crudely. Much too crudely for these modern early dinners that start with lunchtime lighting.'

'Well, military scarlet has character. Here!' I said, unravelling thirty yards and flinging it at her feet.

'My figure is not that of a soldier. I am not padded.'

'Indeed not.' I observed her clothes, hanging lankly on her elegant frame. Frankly, I was at my wits' end to know what to propose next.

'My dear Duchess—tomato?' I started enthusiastically. She interrupted me tartly.

'Your Grace, Mr Hartnell, Your Grace.'

I blushed. Did she expect me to retire to the servants' hall and don a green baize apron? Really, the Duchess was being rather old-fashioned. Did she not realize that in a neighbouring street a Russian prince, ran a smart dress shop, and minor princes were selling ugly knick-knacks to stupid people at outrageous prices?

'What about this one, Your Grace—red hot poker?'

'A very ugly plant. His Grace forbids my gardeners to plant a single one at—.'

'Your Grace, look at this lovely coral chiffon,' I ventured, 'Such a kind and comforting colour.'

'But coral, Mr Hartnell, is for housemaids' necks.'

'Then poppy, Your Grace, poppy,' and I flung a length of poppy coloured stuff across the full length of the room.

'Flanders,' she replied, gazing wistfully out of the window, and I remembered and understood.

It really was becoming more and more difficult. Every flaming tone was here at her disposal, and nothing was coloured right to suit the whim of Her Grace.

'Your Grace—cherry?'

'Ah, cherry. Yes, Mr Hartnell, cherry. That sweetest of blossom, that loveliest of trees. We have avenues of them at—. You must come to see them some time. They are quite beautiful. But not the pink of the blossom, Mr Hartnell, not the pink. *Si j'avais vingt ans*, but no, for me the cherry of cherry ripe. Have you cherry, Mr Hartnell?'

'Of course I have cherry, Your Grace,' I panted, searching wildly amongst all the rolls of material for a chiffon the colour of ripe cherries to suit the dewy-eyed Duchess.

Fixing me with her raised lorgnette, she caused me to stop humming. She returned the lorgnette to her reticule, grasped a wispy length of cherry red chiffon and held it up against her pale face.

'I wonder if I dare,' she murmured, peering into the mirror.

'Oh, of course, Your Grace could,' I replied, full of enthusiasm and tremendously relieved that at last she was pleased with something. 'That is, if perhaps your Grace challenged the colour, if I may use your own phrase, by perhaps a little make-up.'

'Mr Hartnell,' she replied, again using those unnerving lorgnettes, 'I never use make-up. I neither powder nor paint my face. His Grace does not like it. Either I smack or I pinch—like this.'

Her Grace the Duchess of — then improved her complexion with sharp smacking, followed by some cruel pinching between forefinger and thumb. I quickly removed myself on some excuse, leaving Her Grace smacking and pinching until I should imagine she pinched herself not cherry but black and blue.

The next day there was a message from Her Grace to say that she had decided, after all, to have the dress copied in black!

Nowadays, I am most careful to arrange that my home telephone number is ex-directory. Before the war, whether in my Regent's Park house or before that at the flat in Clarges Street, I was constantly bothered and embarrassed by telephone calls after six o'clock in the evenings. These would quite often be personal appeals from husbands anxious to know exactly when they might expect delivery of their wives' dresses. I sympathized with their concern and irritation, but we might have twenty or thirty dresses to deliver by two small delivery vans to Belgravia, Mayfair or Bayswater or up to the heights of Hampstead all at the same hour. It was therefore somewhat difficult for my dispatch department to organize equally-timed distribution.

Ill-advisedly I picked up the telephone one evening to hear an explosion like this from a certain Major:

'Is that Hartnell's? ... it isn't? ... then dammit it ought to be ... What? Who is it speaking? Who? ... Ah! You are the very person I want ... Yes, Sir, indeed you can help me—and at once too ... It's absolutely disgraceful, Sir. Here are my wife and I still waiting for the dress to arrive ... What, you don't know when? Well, damn well find out, Sir ... D'you hear? ... Absolutely appalling ... My wife has been all the morning having massage—two hours at Antoine having her hair and nails done. Now, Sir, no damn dress! And we are due to go to a big diplomatic reception tonight. Kindly find out from your shop when we can expect the dress and ring me back here at Grosvenor House. Do you hear, Sir!'

He slammed down his receiver. By a fluke I managed to establish contact with the dispatch department and learned that the dress had been delivered, and rang through to the Major to acquaint him of this happy fact.

'Oh, I say, Hartnell,' he responded, much mollified. 'How awfully decent of you to let me know ... Yes, old boy, the dress has arrived and it's absolutely stunning ... thanks most awfully ... I say, Hartnell, I am very sorry I was so snappy on the wire a little while ago. But, you know, it is sort of rather maddening for a man having his wife stumping up and down the flat here for the last two hours in nothing but her tiara and knickers!'

The galloping Major was lamblike, however, compared with the Hon. Mrs M. who sought my advice upon the style of dress that would most become her when she attended a Drawing Room at Buckingham Palace, for presentation at Court, sometime in May.

She had been extremely hard to please and had tried on numerous dresses, scribbling many hurried notes in the back of her diary on the neckline, hemline and waistline of each dress. She made little sketches, I noted, adding to them spasmodic remarks in pencil such as 'good', 'remember this', 'could be mixed', 'splendid', 'pretty-ish', 'regal', 'just me', 'distinctive'. Although she came to no final decision, she asked if I would send patterns of all the materials to her house in a respectable but somewhat dingy street at the back of Kensington:

A worried and unsettled woman, smoking cigarettes consecutively, she kept shaking her head as she spoke. She was swarthy of complexion, thin as a bone and seemed very unsure of herself but there was still a fine manner about her. Thanking me in a few clipped sentences for all my time and trouble, she went away in a hurry.

This strange interview was sharply recalled when, some weeks later, the carriage attendant told me that the Hon. Mrs M. had arrived at the front door in a taxicab and would not get out of it until I came to the pavement edge to assist her.

So, in the sharp sunlight of a spring mid-morning, any passer-by could have seen me helping the Hon. Mrs M., arrayed in full Court dress, to alight from her taxicab. I followed her up the staircase until we reached the showroom on the first floor.

Upon her alarming entrance, a tactful mother from the Shires quickly ushered her schoolboy son and little daughter to the privacy of a convenient fitting room. Some inexperienced English junior assistants hurried from the room, tittering, while the more stalwart Parisienne *vendeuses* stood by me during what promised to be an embarrassing quarter of an hour.

While waiting for an explanation of her grotesque attire, I offered her a cigarette which she accepted eagerly. I lit it for her through the trembling fingers of her long kid gloves, which were old and crackled, distinctly dirty at the finger tips and still smelled strongly of benzine.

'I thought you would like to see me in my Court dress,' she began, 'I have not forgotten how very helpful you were about it. Really, most kind! But, alas, I realized after all that I could not afford to buy one from you, so I have made it myself. But I thought it was only fair to you to let you see it after all the trouble you took. I do hope you like it. Do you?'

Flicking her ash on my carpet, she walked a few paces, paused, jerked her head several times and spoke again.

'The train belonged to my grandmother, Lady —, and of course it's not very new.'

We agreed unanimously that the train definitely did not look outstandingly new. It was of a silver metallic material, brown with tarnish and curling at the edges. A discarded sardine tin was what it immediately brought to mind. Strips of this awful metal stuff had apparently been cut from the sides of the Court train and inserted at intervals on a skirt which had been made up from the length of the patterns that we had sent to her, giving an effect of patchwork quilt behind prison bars. Lumps of material in different textures and colouring had been sewn together, ignoring any pattern or design.

All the time she was waggling a fan of about five ostrich feathers, each plume uncurled and stiff. They were dyed in five different colours, deep mauve, china blue, peach, saffron and grass.

'I also made this fan myself, together with the dress, but it is all inspired by *you*, Mr Hartnell. Of course, I shall tell everybody that you made it. It is only what you deserve!' She paused. 'Of course we can arrange to put your name as designer in the papers, can't we, with a full description underneath my name. Does everybody here like it?' She glanced round. We all felt too sick to answer.

'Won't you sit down, Madam?' someone suggested, playing for time, while we considered how gracefully to get rid of this bizarre woman.

'Yes, it suits very well.' Whereupon she suddenly sat down heavily on a poor little squeaking chair and some of her stitching split.

Jerking her head forward several times like a hen about to peck, she adjured us to admire her tiara—another horrible, home-made affair. It was of oxidized lace and steel wire and sewn along the top was a chain of cheap diamanté, punctured at odd intervals with upstanding imitation pearls, like nuts on a trifle. Some old Court plumes held a length of crumpled cream tulle, and wisps of unruly hair escaped from her dank bun.

Rising to her full height, which was not very great, she made a tremendous sweeping gesture with her right arm, landing the outstretched fan behind her head like Dorothy Ward used to do so beautifully, which Beatrice Lillie does so amusingly, and fan dancers continue to do professionally.

'This is the effect I like best.' She threw back her head, opened her mouth sideways and laughed to herself for quite a while. Meanwhile, a party of extremely attractive women entered the showroom, took one look at this extraordinary figure, still laughing, and scuttled away. I feel sure they all went straight round to Worth to place the orders for their Court dresses.

Very tenderly, Madame Jeanne approached Mrs M.

'Madam,' she begged, 'we all have much to do this morning. We cannot wait here any longer. Your dress is very cleverly made but, perhaps, Madam, it might be better if you would permit us to lend you one just a little more suitable for the occasion ?'

'Oh, what an excellent suggestion.' I added, 'That's if Mrs M. will warn us as to which Court she is attending.'

'I have not heard from the Lord Chamberlain yet,' she snapped, jerking her head again, as the laugh disappeared from her wild face. 'In any case, I shall wear *this* dress. I feel it is *me*, and, of course, *you*, Mr Hartnell, and I promise to send you a photograph of myself in it.'

We guided her to the door and down the stairs. None of us had the courage to escort her across the pavement. The carriage attendant did so and courteously helped her into a taxicab that most fortunately was passing as we emerged.

'Where to, Madam?'

'The Ritz, driver.'

Now the lady would be the responsibility of the Ritz Hotel, unless perchance she redirected the driver to her own address.

I received the promised photograph. Perhaps it still stands on her piano as a predominating *objet de vertu* in her Kensington drawing-room.

Sad to record, the name of the Hon. Mrs M. did not appear, after all, in the list of ladies presented at Court.

A few weeks after taking the house at number 26 Bruton Street, I sat down to write a most fateful letter.

Early in the autumn of 1935 the engagement was announced of His Royal Highness the Duke of Gloucester to Lady Alice Montagu-Douglas-Scott, daughter of the 7th Duke of Buccleuch. This was the third of King George V's sons to marry, and just a year before the Duke of Kent had been wedded to the lovely Princess Marina of Greece.

The excitement and romantic flavour of this second Royal betrothal encouraged me to write on my new notepaper, of which

I was very proud, to Lady Alice, asking if I might be permitted to submit some ideas for her wedding dress.

The answer came back from Drumlanrig Castle in Dumfriesshire. It was written with a directness which I found later to be characteristic. The letter which I still cherish said that Lady Alice would call and see me when she returned to London the following week.

I was delighted, of course, but at that moment had no idea that the bridesmaids would include Their Royal Highnesses the young Princesses. I did not realize at the time that Lady Alice's promised visit was to mark the turning point in my career.

— CHAPTER SEVEN —

In retrospect the mind's eye is inclined to light upon the great moments and to overlook the quiet monotones of one's working days. The pieces click too neatly into the jigsaw. Before I record what followed upon that very gracious letter from Lady Alice it may be of interest to explain something of the organization and mechanism of a house like mine. It is an aspect of a *couturier's* life which is often overlooked by the general public, who, naturally enough, only see sketches or photographs of the completed dresses or, more rarely, the glamorous women who wear them.

I employ at the moment in Bruton Street and Bruton Place a staff of 385 persons. Most members of the senior staff are brought from Paris, since there exists a gentleman's agreement in London not to entice away one another's leading employees. At least, this exists between the members of the Incorporated Society of London Fashion Designers though some of us, including myself, have been guilty of breaking it!

Then a business manager, a house manager, a showroom manageress, a receptionist, and assistant saleswomen are required. In addition, there are office staff and secretaries, stock-keepers and stockroom staff, housekeeper, canteen manageress and canteen cooks, cleaning women, telephonists, packers, delivery men, a carriage attendant, a day watchman and a night watchman.

Let us start with the much-photographed models. Choosing a model is a most invidious duty. Whenever a young woman presents herself for this work, I always make a point of seeing her personally. Which of us suffers the greater embarrassment during these interviews I am not certain.

The unfortunate girl, wearing one of the less successful current model dresses, is made to parade up and down the Salons, quizzed by the rest of the showroom staff as though she were some captured insect, whilst my *Directrice de Salon* asks some very pertinent questions and assesses her anatomical measurements in a most callous way.

Meanwhile, I regard her reflection in a mirror. The points I look for are poise, walk and silhouette, and if she fulfils these requirements she cannot but have an air of distinction, too. Many a duchess would like to look as my mannequins look.

A pretty face is the least essential of attributes. With every modern aid to beauty, an intelligent mannequin can, by creating her own style in coiffure, *maquillage* and adornment, acquire enough beauty, however synthetic.

If a mannequin is truly and photogenically beautiful, she does not stay very long in any dressmaker's employment. The luxurious fashion magazines, constantly searching for new photographic models, entice these girls away with a promise of much higher payment for posing in a few dresses, hats or fur coats than they receive for working unceasingly throughout each day of each week of each season in a *maison de couture*.

Mannequins are to a designer what actresses are to a playwright, except that they have no star quality. But they can bring delight or despair to the originator, for they can make or mar what they are asked to interpret. One has had disappointment, of course, but I shall always be grateful to the galaxy of young women who have given beauty and grace to so many of my dresses throughout the years. I am tempted to mention them all by name. Many are now women of title or the wives of millionaires, bankers, country squires, police inspectors, politicians, rich men, poor men ...

From the tumultuous 'thirties I remember with gratitude Joyce Page, always known as 'Page', the first wife of my great friend, Robert Nesbitt, the young London theatrical producer. It was impossible to put any clothes on her that were not of impeccable taste. For one thing, she always insisted on being shown my designs before they were made on her. If she did not entirely approve of both material and style, I would alter the sketches. If the finished dress did not live up to her own standard of streamlined elegance, she would gently refuse to wear it. She was as thin as a toothpick and moved with the agility of some fleet-footed deer. She scraped back her tinted golden hair into a huge cluster of curls and had violet eyelids powdered with silver dust.

All her dresses were black and white. Escorted by her husband and myself, she dressed herself up as my *mannequin de luxe*, and we visited the Grandes Semaines at Deauville and Le Touquet. She would appear in the Casino and the restaurants wearing her *ensembles* of black and white. A fabulous evening coat of sleek black ermine would be slipped over, or slipped off, a sheath dress of black *ciré* chiffon. White satin, printed with gigantic black poppies—each flower head loaded with the laudanum of jet embroideries—was a dress that gleamed beneath a ground length cape of black organza. A stiff white cotton *pique* evening dress was hemmed with black fur, and her tall figure was halved by a tailored skirt of glittering black sequins and a solid sequin Eton jacket of glistening white. That caress was called 'Manslaughter'.

Around her flocked the French fashion photographers, but on inquiring the name of the designer and finding it was an unknown Hartnell instead of the more conspicuous Chanel, they clamped down their shutters and scampered away.

Then Fritzi, the beauty queen of Berlin, came my way. She was the best mannequin I think I ever had. Fritzi was tall, lissom and lovely, a symphony in tones of brown. Her hair was mahogany brown and glossy. Her eyes were brown, and her skin a soft golden brown. It was on Fritzi that I first designed a whole collection of brown evening dresses which, at first disapproved of by my 'black-minded' customers, were at last accepted warmly. It gave them a further opportunity to wear their cherished brown mink coats, wraps and stoles at night with these brown evening dresses.

Patsey was the 'good style' girl. She was of such transcendental good style that in fact she finished up by having no style at all. Demure and *distinguée*, with grey eyes and mousey hair, everybody liked whatever she wore. She was the very mirror of their own style. She wore grey flannel suits, grey afternoon dresses, grey velvet hostess gowns, grey chiffon dinner dresses, and a chinchilla cape for comic relief. Grey pearls, of course, and a cut-steel regimental brooch set in a medium-sized grey felt hat.

A blazing blonde was Suzanne Piatt, a natural platinum blonde. She had square shoulders and the figure of a young athlete, and to all the pastels I made for her she added her blonde brilliance.

To counteract all this black, brown, grey and pastel, I weakened under the highly-coloured presence of Avril Anstruther. I engaged her on the spot. I have never loaded so many jewels and silver fox furs on the frame of one woman as I have done on the vibrant Avril. Inch square sapphires would be stuck like Eastern mosaic all over a lemon wool evening coat. Prussian blue cloth would become stiff with magenta spangles, cherries and rubies. An innocent enough mustard velvet jacket was no good to Miss Avril unless it clanked with turquoise *cabochons*, zircons and scarabs. Wearing this dazzling coat over a slim turquoise dress, she would prevail upon me to embroider the dress with yellow china beads, amber and gold.

Jewellery had to be specially designed. Beautiful modern costume jewellery was specially made in Paris, and Avril would select for herself three-strand necklaces and five-strand bracelets of brightest turquoise, cut into square-shaped hunks and fastened with clattering gilt.

It was Avril who first proved to me the elegance of purple for the younger woman. I remembered seeing the beautiful Queen Alexandra, one of my boyhood heroines, in violet cloth, violet sequined dresses and sable stoles stabbed with clusters of Russian violets; and I retained a sweet memory of my maternal grandmother in stiff violet brocade topped by a small bonnet of parma violets, tied with violet velvet ribbons. I had always associated this colour with the grey-haired years of maturity and as the prerogative of grandmothers.

On Miss Avril, with her wide-set eyes, cream skin and coffee-coloured hair, these violet symphonies sang a different tune. Violet became the season's most fashionable colour. Amongst the dresses I made for her were—Purple Past, Violent Violet, Pure Though Purple, Mauve Moment, Violet Ray, Modest Violet and Ultra Violet;

the very naming of these models being indicative of the sudden violet vogue of that time.

I hesitate to consider how many small wild animals have sacrificed their lives and furry skins in the embellishment of Miss Avril. Hundreds of ermines and minks, dozens of foxes, white, black, silver, red and cross, countless rabbits, monkeys and skunks died in the cause of *haute fourrure*. But they seemed to glow and bristle in a kind of reincarnation around those friendly shoulders. She might fling them with callous abandon around her neck, or trail them along the showroom carpet with apparent disdain, but, on returning to the models' room, she would hang them carefully on the fur rack and, stroking them with her claw-tipped fingers, would press them lovingly against her cheek, murmuring, 'Oh, you darlings—you darlings.'

Dolores, the reigning figure in my *cabine des mannequins*, has reigned there for many years, but age does not seem to impair her. She takes delight in arriving every morning looking almost frightening without a speck of make-up, to emerge at ten o'clock in full rig like a butterfly escaped from its chrysalis. Her funny face becomes heavy with cosmetics, and the wisps of black hair have been augmented by a strapping plait and a hefty bun of jet black hair, which I bought for her at some expense. She is a dress-actress, and every garment she wears, whether it is 'White Sepulchre' or 'Carmen's Cousin', is invested with a sense of drama all her own.

Jane is a frail beauty, as fresh and pink as apple blossom; Lana a milkmaid or a full-blown rose; Elizabeth, neat as a piri in her close-cut tweeds; while Cynthia and Cassandra look splendid in everything.

I owe much to these decorative young women, whose elegant support is indispensable to any designer of dress, and they have been a source of inspiration to me in more ways than one. One morning, watching a parade I decided to create a scent of my own imagining. It is a most fascinating subject and I could not rest until I had gone to the ancient town of Grasse, on the slopes above the southern coast of France. My guide was a delightful Frenchman, M. Leon Chiris, who, led me around the famous perfume factories started by his family some centuries ago, and showed me field after field fragrant with blossom.

I sensed rather than knew what I was seeking. At the turn of the nineteenth century, modern women were content to use very light waters such as lavender, jasmine or maidenhair fern. It was only in the tasteless twenties of this century that there was an urge for stronger scents to be worn with some of the ugliest fashions in history. Heavy and clumsy perfumes were produced, but neither the scents nor the fashions were appreciated by the men.

I was eager to produce a fragrance of present-day modernism, yet overtoned with a clear and lingering loveliness that should become the light complexioned women of England and subtly convey an aura of youth. I was advised to mingle the scent of all the white flowers. So cartloads of lovely blossoms of jasmine, lilies of the valley, white hyacinths, white lilac and the fragile tuberose were tipped into the copper cauldrons. I made several visits to the chemical laboratories and at last enjoyed the final distillation of the fragrance. It was exactly what I had so long sought, but the name remained elusive.

The charming Madame Chiris settled it for me.

'Oh, with this so lovely scent I am in love,' she exclaimed.

'*Merci*, Madame,' I replied, 'I shall call my perfume "In Love".'

— CHAPTER EIGHT —

Early in my career, I had discovered the importance of developing a kind of mental division of ideas. While considering the delicate arts of perfumery I may suddenly find myself involved in other complicated aspects of my business. The exacting and most important task of designing a collection demands, in particular, a kind of split personality, for one must carry on with everyday routine while planning far ahead in terms of time, climate and taste.

In the full heat of summer I try to become enthusiastic over the heavy-weight woollens and student tweeds which may figure in the autumn and winter designs. The winter collection must, moreover, include light dresses for those fortunate women who plan to winter abroad. It must be ready for showing to the Press and overseas buyers by the last week in July, which means preparing as early as April or May.

Each spring my stock-keeper, Miss Louie, warns me that appointments are being made with the travellers or agents of all the leading textile manufacturers in England, Scotland, France, Italy and Switzerland.

In a working studio, equipped for the selection of daytime and evening materials, I look for what is new in texture and design. I see the woollens first, because I enjoy them least. They will be made up into perfect tailor-made suits, I hope, but I always feel a trifle frustrated by the classic limitations of tailored clothes.

The first collection of woollens arrives. Four or five suitcases from a famous house are unstrapped and let loose countless swatches of masculine-looking suitings which, however, make up admirably for the ladies when adroitly tailored. I am allowed to keep this collection for half a day only, as other houses are waiting their turn to see it.

Rival representatives pass each other on the staircase of my trade entrance and hundreds more tweeds are placed on another table. We go through these two collections quickly, comparing the various points of colour and weight.

A nutbrown partnership of thick wool and thin wool dyed to exactly matching colour may be chosen here; and there, possibly, a heavy coating of prune colour to go over a dress of strawberry pink crepe which we shall have to find later amongst the silks. The next travellers call round in the afternoon, and soon we have made a choice of about eight woollen samples and have packed away the first two collections to make room for the new arrivals.

The afternoon is spent searching through all the patterns in every swatch. If another tan-coloured wool is found to be more suitable than our first choice, we promptly cancel the earlier one.

Huge cases of brilliantly coloured woollens arrive from France. All these are carefully scrutinized and compared again with the earlier collections, while a careful note is made of comparative prices and the promised dates for delivery.

By now I have spent about two or three days struggling through the heaviest of tweeds and am longing for the relief of lighter woollens which are always a delight to me. Little check woollens of, say, grey and white are teamed up with the plain woollens to match in similar grey, and there is a whole range of colourings from which to choose.

Now arrives a delectable selection of coat fabrics and jewel-coloured velours and duvetyns. These are for the dressy coats to be worn, perhaps, over dresses of dark satin or cocktail frocks of chestnut and gold brocade. But I must exercise self-control, for already I have chosen materials for many a model, and the collection must not become too overloaded with woollen coats.

The next collection is brought to me; exquisitely soft cloths from which we select a cosy wool of mint green to be trimmed with beaver, a blood red duvetyn to be weighted with black Persian lamb, and a brilliant cherry wool to be collared and cuffed with snowy white mink, taking good care that, when the model is finished, the mannequin does not look too much like Father Christmas. For here, in this winter collection, the art of the furrier is combined with that of the dressmaker. I invite, therefore, my master furrier, Signor Belloni, known as Mr Bell, to estimate the cost of such luxurious pelts as embellishment to the *ensembles* and, of course, I receive the expert advice I need on furs.

Then follows a session with three masters: Mr Bell, and the famous tailors, Signor Rossi and Monsieur François, who help me select the correct quality of velvets for winter wearing. The quality they will choose; and I, the colouring.

With the selection of velvets, the viewing of the silken goods has begun. In small patterns, a few inches square, are all the translucent colours of a stained glass window. Each suggests to me the lovely coat or dress that might be created, but another voice, that of an unreasoning customer, also speaks from the wings.

'It's disgraceful that this expensive velvet dress should crease.' They do, of course, crease, and always will. But is there not always an iron?

The pastel shades of velvet are almost irresistible in palest turquoise, lilac and candy pink, but resisted they are, for they would prove too costly for the young wearer and too enlargening for the mature.

Some exquisite silks and satins are rippled out at our feet and the temptation is to buy the whole lot, but common sense enters to resist the rustling flower-strewn taffetas and metal-threaded brocades, often too rich in beauty for women to wear. I have to remember reluctantly that at my dress collections a woman may refuse the most beautiful dress in preference for a little workaday number. Recklessly, however, I do order one or two of these glorious products, to be included in the collection merely for the sake of decoration and personal satisfaction.

There seems to be no end to the treasures; rainbow-hued taffetas and organzas, sometimes printed in exactly the same design, and vaporous gleaming gauzes; coloured crepes and lustrous satins tinted to perfection; materials for the linings, petticoats and under-dresses. Then come the laces, usually based on well-known classic designs such as have been woven on Nottingham looms for years. Another collection of lace presents a formidable task; whether loaded with tinsel or light as a tinted cobweb.

One cannot possibly order a lengthy yardage of these gorgeous laces because one has to cut in half a single yard of the opulent *dentelle*, costing £18 a yard of 18 in. width. Only one of these half-yards will be used to compose the sparse bodice of an evening dress, and the skirt will be clouds of infinite tulle.

The indispensable accessories include belts of leather or material. Buttons of every conceivable shape and composition. Gigantic boxes arrive crammed with perfectly imitated flowers and scores of cards on which are sewn dazzling beads and jewels.

From most of these great houses of supply I receive, within a few days, an 'illustrated copy', which is a sheet of paper, a business document, on which are pasted small patterns to remind me what I have ordered. The design and colour of many other materials now shown I must commit to memory, and having returned to the quiet of the country I then settle down to the sketching of the imagined models. It is the month of May and my drawing board is empty. I have some ten weeks to create about a hundred models.

There are some designers who, with the chosen stuffs at hand, begin to drape almost directly on to their mannequins. This has never been my method for half the pleasure and pride of my craft is the drawing of each model before it is ever seen in the workrooms.

In most cases I know exactly what to draw and which mannequin will wear the model. While viewing the multitude of materials, I pause to appreciate and then order a length of any specific stuff. At that moment an appropriate design usually suggests itself and I pigeonhole it in my mind.

Therefore I draw the certainties first. The boldly-charactered tweeds of large check or dominant stripe compel the designer to arrange them in obvious composition. The patterned brocades and printed silks give a little more licence, depending mainly on the cut and shape. The classic plain materials, which I draw last, offer scope for free designing and embellishment upon an inviting blank canvas.

It would be tedious to describe the plotting of each of the imagined hundred models. My house in Windsor Forest becomes a studio and I wander from room to room. At eleven o'clock I am in the morning room, furnished mostly in carved pine wood with coral velvet hangings, and there I picture the morning suits. Promptly I sit down at the large wooden desk, place in front of me the samples of materials, and draw them as I imagine them to be worn. Woollen morning suits, pleated or plain, with flared or belted topcoats, appear on my sketch block, many of the leather belts I ordered being used up in the process.

In the afternoon I go upstairs to the small white-washed studio and paint the sketches in the allotted colours. The accessories of hats, gloves, shoes and handbags are drawn unconsciously, harmonizing with each design.

If I give a small dinner party at this time, I cannot avoid appraising the appearance of my women guests. It sometimes helps to remind me in the morning how better to manipulate all that paraphernalia of velvet, satin and mink.

At other times, in my pale-coloured drawing-room, I pin lengths of gold tissue to the curtains, watching the fold and grace of the falling stuff, and throw coloured satin across two cushions on the sofa, imagining them to be bust and hips respectively.

This effect is not always a happy one!

Often I have to wait until they can be correctly manipulated, back in London, on one of the willowy figures of my mannequins before I secure the desired result.

I need to telephone constantly to London inquiring if the goods from Paris have arrived and requesting my stock-keeper to send down by car great rolls of fabric and furs, and bags of embroidery jewels. It is impossible for me to try to work in London because of the interruptions and distractions. Only by being alone and unworried can I complete the sketches of the hundredfold collection.

Inspiration is unconscious, or perhaps subconscious. The dresses in the pictures of the great painters are often in my mind; the Italian masters for purest line, and all the French fun of Boucher, Watteau and Madame Vigee le Brun; Fragonard for the *folies de grandeur*; and later Gavarni, with Renoir and Tissot for a touch of *chichi*.

The drawings of Drian, Bakst, Sutherland, Cecil Beaton and Ronald Searle may help. Even common objects such as a slithering sardine or the steel bright lines of a railway station can stimulate ideas if a silver reception gown is wanted.

Who can say exactly what gives rise to creative impulse? A lingering melody or the cloying scent of lilies may suggest a romantic mauve dress for a sentimental matron. A wax-white magnolia in the moonlight is a debutante dancing at Hurlingham. Swans on the lake may turn into young women in white arriving to cut a cake at Queen Charlotte's Ball, and a farmyard is redolent of sporting tweeds.

Intending to draw one design I sketch firstly the head, then roughly the limbs of the figure, turning the body towards its right, so that the left hip is foremost to my view. The left hip is the focal point of nearly all draperies, clumps of flowers, panels, buddings, sashes or bows. Then the arms, one akimbo and one outstretched, to allow for the arrangement of the sleeves. Finally, I draw the feet.

The line of the neck of the dress is inscribed, and remembering that a belt may cut across to mark the waistline, my pencil slips down the centre of the figure and it goes on towards the left hip.

In designing an evening dress, my pencil may flow extravagantly down to the tiptoe, and then perhaps trail out further along the floor level; but the further my pencil travels towards the corners of the page, the more will be the ultimate cost of this dress. So I have to erase this artistic flourish and reluctantly put the flow of the skirt to the dictates of modern mediocrity.

Here, then, is the line of a full-length dress in some stiffish material, the duck egg blue satin from Ducharne that delineates a seaming from the right of the bust across the waistline to the left flank. That line can be strengthened by a draped scarf of the satin that swathes the corsage complete, circles round the back, is moulded over the figure and cascades to the ground in a gathered side panel. It can be partnered by another swathing from right to left or lined with a contrasting colour, *rose du barri*, citron or black velvet.

The panels could be cut longer, swagged round to behind the hips, looped through a satin, tailored or jewelled belt, and then let fall in bustled line to form two peacock trains. The whole dress might look just as fine in the rose and gold brocade from Bianchini, or the plainest of black paper taffeta. I hastily paint all the varying versions of this one original dress, from which I soon have six different dresses suggested to me by the one basic drawing. In my mind I allocate the dresses to each of my six mannequins, respective of figure, type and colouring, but always nervously aware of what is known as 'casual calamities', when my best model girls either want to go somewhere else, become a freelance model, get married or expect a baby.

On second thoughts, the pale blue satin dress may appear a little weak in character, and I consider that this could become one of the *grandes robes* of the collection, if it were enriched with Hartnell embroideries. For the sake of contrast it could be embroidered in the blue-black of sphinx-coloured beads, or several tones of rose pink, or nothing but the sparkle of silver.

Blue is always the husband's favourite, so I undo the jewel bags and clutter the table with every kind of blue bead I can find. Star sapphires, aquamarines, turquoises, zircons and ice-blue diamonds glint and glitter. I base them on the form of a cornflower, or a scabious or cluster of plumbago in a mist of blue forget-me-nots. Smoothing out a glabrous portion of the clear blue satin, I jostle it gently into position with the tip of my pencil.

Then comes an actual life-size drawing of this glittering cluster which, when expertly embroidered, may vie with the jewelled *chefs d'œuvre* of Van Cleef and Arpels and Benvenuto Cellini.

The dress design must now be painted. On my palette I squeeze out cerulean blue, with a dash of viridian green and a large helping of Chinese white which, with much water, makes a perfect basis for an aquamarine blue wash. The sable-haired paintbrush splashes the watery blue into the panelled drapes of satin leaving dry highlights where necessary, and then adding deeper blue into the denser folds.

When the painting has dried, with a sharp pencil I draw in detail the trailing design for the embroideries, perhaps leaving the swathed material plain but patterning the rest of the dress in graduated entirety. Each motif is then stressed with solid blue paint and each flower, bud, leaf and tendril finally illuminated with thick spotting of body white.

It occurs to me to evolve further embroideries of differing designs in tones of emerald, *peridot*, jade and silver to go on white satin; tortoiseshell, topaz and amber on blonde satin; or rubies, rose diamonds or tourmalines on pink satin. So I draw and paint three more.

Over the white satin with its green embroideries I draw a long stole of snow-white fox lined with emerald velvet. To the pink is added a tight-fitting jacket of cerise wool. And the amber and gold becomes long-sleeved, with the wrists and low-cut bodice bordered with dark brown mink. Altogether I produce about forty designs for embroidered dresses of velvet, satin or tulle, from which I choose and make up about thirty.

I then do a series of plain dresses—draped jersey, hand-tucked chiffon and floating organza. A set of black dresses is always a necessity, little straight ones for the day, or crisply-cut short black taffetas, or stiff satin peppered with jet for the cocktail hour.

The winter collection is not complete without furs, so I draw ideas and shapes for full-length coats, capes, boleros and stoles in inky sable and slinky mink.

On returning to my business house I discuss all these designs with my *premières*, tailors and head *vendeuses*, whose opinions I value highly. The lengths of lovely materials are chopped up and handed out to each workroom.

After a few days we begin the innumerable fittings, hour after hour, and day by day, upon the patient mannequins. The charming Madame Claude St Cyr flies over from Paris to see the models and create appropriate hats. And my friend, Edward Rayne, most obligingly designs special shoes.

The naming of the dresses is my duty, too, and I find this twice-yearly nomenclature a little trying. I recall that Madame Lucille used to indulge in the most fanciful names, exotic and erotic, but I lean towards the more common-sense and modern phrase. I shall never again use the titles 'Fading Flower' and 'Not Quite Me', for they were not copied once; perhaps because of some psychological impact on the ladies; or maybe they were just bad dresses. 'Nothing Much' and 'Mousie' also failed ingloriously though 'Belle of the Ball' and 'Colonel's Lady' were sure-fire in Sloane Square and Cheltenham.

The last rite, before showing to the Press, the buyers and the public, is the dress rehearsal. On this occasion I always suffer for, in spite of the tremendous help from all the members of my working staff, I feel somehow dissatisfied with the display, sensing either too much flamboyance or insignificance. Fortunately, dresses are mutable and can be changed around. We turn them back to front, chop a long dress to the length of a ballet dress, hiding it underneath a mink coat, or forbidding the poor model girl ever to wear it again.

Suddenly one of my vigilant *vendeuses* may exclaim: 'But that is almost exactly like Balmain's new white dress.' If true, the dress must of course, be eliminated, although the similarity has not been intentional.

Influences are, however, inevitable. Much as I would enjoy seeing all the collections of the lovely clothes of the Paris dressmakers, I do not go. For one thing I have not been invited, except by the gracious Christian Dior, and it would be impossible to resist the temptation of emulating or including in one's own collection, not a copy, but an echo perhaps, of the novelty of line, manner or mood.

It is plagiarism of a very different order that becomes a nightmare to designers. I remember making for Isabel Jeans an apricot chiffon evening dress that brought me, and others, a small fortune. It was the kind of dress every woman then wanted; a mixture of sophistication and femininity, finely handtucked, fitting the figure, yet floating vaporously in movement. In *The Man in Possession* Isabel wore it with superb grace as she drifted around the stage to dissuade a hostile bailiff, Raymond Massey, from his intentions.

I copied this dress by the hundred and so, apparently, did other dressmakers. One night at the Embassy Club I counted about eighteen of these same chiffon dresses on the dance floor at once. I recognized the wearers of about half of them, who smiled sweetly, but the wearers whom I did not recognize looked away in embarrassment. The explanation was that the former had ordered original dresses directly from my firm, whereas the others were wearing pirated copies made by some other dressmaker or the handy 'little woman round the corner'.

It happens like this. Let us say Madame X of Knightsbridge is sitting in the front row of the stalls and admires the dress so elegantly worn by Isabel Jeans. Anxious to reproduce it in her own dress shop, she visits the theatre again with notebook, pencil and powerful opera glasses.

If not quite successful in committing to memory all the details, she may send in her sister, her best friend, or head fitter, wearing Madame's own mink coat and diamonds, to my salon in Bruton Street to take an even closer and longer view of Miss Jeans' model dress. Furthermore, Madame X has given her representative clear instructions that if she is still uncertain she may actually order, fit and purchase a copy of the coveted garment.

Home it goes, this finished dress, to a private house in the suburbs whence it is immediately forwarded to Madame's shop at Knightsbridge. Here it is quickly copied—badly but cheaply—for the clients of Madame's Maison. Thus, a few weeks later, sitting in the Embassy, I see these *moitié-moitié* models of my original and Madame's copy.

After the work that goes into the creation of a model this kind of thing is most irritating, but unhappily there is no law to protect us from plagiarism and piracy. My friend Edward Molyneux suffered likewise from the ruthless copying of his models. On one occasion he appealed to the law and lost his case, at considerable cost, thereby giving a free licence to the copyists to continue the malpractice.

It is worth noting that the French Government stands staunchly behind the *couturiers* of Paris who have organized a corporate society called *La Chambre Syndicate de la Couture Parisienne*. People who offend against this body of far-sighted gentlemen are sent to prison, a procedure of which I thoroughly approve.

— PART TWO —
THE FULFILMENT

— CHAPTER NINE —

When Lady Alice Scott wrote to me from Drumlanrig Castle I had no idea, of course, that one of her young bridesmaids was destined to be the Queen of England, and that I would have the honour of designing her Coronation robes.

Lady Alice arrived, quietly dressed in a brown tweed suit. I noticed her beautifully moulded cheek bones and the smile which someone has described as 'like that of a forest gnome'. She came with her sister, Lady Sybil Phipps, and I showed some of my current collection. She quickly selected a few dresses for her trousseau and gave her views on the wedding dress, which was to be of a strict simplicity.

The wedding was to be in Westminster Abbey in November, 1935. Because of the dim lighting in the Abbey it was considered that the dress should not be in stark white, but in a soft tone with something of the glimmer of pearl. The ladies of the Buccleuch family were opposed to lace for Lady Alice's wedding veil. This pleased me for an antique bridal lace veil, extracted once a year from a grandmother's treasure chest and quickly replaced amidst sachets of lavender, rarely enhances the appearance of any bride. Lace, hanging lank and discoloured with age on each side of the face, resembles some attenuated judge's wig, contrasting ill with a young girl's beauty. A drifting cloud of crisp modern tulle is much more becoming, falling from a circle of blossom or from a sparkling tiara.

A shadow was unhappily cast over the wedding, for the Duke of Buccleuch died. In consequence the marriage ceremony was to be held in the privacy of the Chapel Royal at Buckingham Palace.

Meanwhile, there arose the question of designs for the bridesmaids. I drew and painted a variety of sketches, being careful that, if there should happen to be some very young girls, their dress would harmonize with the older ones. I can confess now that this was what

I hoped would prove a piece of intelligent anticipation. Surely the Duke of Gloucester's two little nieces would be among those chosen.

Early in October the names of the eight bridesmaids were announced, probably the youngest eight on record, for seven of them were under seventeen years old; Princess Elizabeth with Princess Margaret Rose, Lady Mary Cambridge, Lady Elizabeth Scott, Lady Angela Scott, Miss Moyra Eileen Scott, Miss Ann Hawkins, Miss Claire Phipps.

The approved sketch for all the bridesmaids showed them wearing something in the nature of a sophisticated Empire style dress, clinging and long-skirted. But Lady Alice confided to me that the Princesses' grandfather, King George V, wished that the little ones should wear girlish dresses. So their frocks were made short. They were of palest pink satin; short skirts bordered with three graduating bands of ruched pink tulle, tiny sleeves and a tulle-bordered bodice.

Later, when I was informed that Her Royal Highness the Duchess of York, accompanied by Their Royal Highnesses Princess Elizabeth and Princess Margaret Rose, would be honouring me with a visit to supervise the first dress fittings for the young Princesses, my staff and I were enthralled in anticipation of this first Royal visit, and I rehearsed them in curtsying.

'Not so quick and jerky. Not like a pecking sparrow, more like a swooning swan,' I entreated.

The Royal ladies arrived a little earlier than expected and, instead of being on the pavement edge to receive them, I was upstairs when they made their entry.

I am glad in a way that I was guilty of this slight error of behaviour, for my first sight of them was a truly enchanting vision and one which I shall never forget. As I moved forward to greet them, all the women in the room rose as one and tendered a lingering curtsy. It was in itself a beautiful and moving sight.

Her Royal Highness the Duchess of York was in silver grey georgette, clouded with the palest grey fox, and her jewels were dew drop diamonds and aquamarines.

The young Princesses, on each side of her, as she led them by the hand, wore little blue jackets, silver buttoned, and tiny grey hats wreathed in blue forget-me-nots, making a symphony of silver and blue.

I thought it my duty to guide them at once through the rather crowded showroom to the privacy of a small room specially set apart for them in the rear of the building. But I noticed then, for the first time, the intentionally measured and deliberate pace of Royal ladies. With lovely smile and gracious movement the Duchess of York acknowledged on either side the reverences of the women present and very slowly moved on and out of sight.

Our future Queen and her sister, then both very young, seemed more interested in the scintillating cars that purred in the mews outside the window, than in their frocks.

The Duchess, meanwhile, asked to see the collection. As a mannequin displayed her dress, the Duchess put the girl at her ease, making a point of appreciating each gown in turn.

I noticed then, and later, that nothing by her is ever belittled and no feelings are hurt. Each offering, however humble, receives a word of appreciation, always understanding, from a mind most well-informed.

Afterwards, I received a summons to the Palace to be in attendance in the Throne Room where the wedding photographs were to be taken. I was standing quietly at the far end of this great room by the side of Mr Hay Wrightson, the well-known photographer, when there entered the bride and bridegroom and to my amazement every other member of the Royal Family.

'Would you please go forward and arrange the Duchess's veil?' a page murmured to me. I walked forward, made a bow and knelt to disentangle the bride's tulle veil from the spur of the Duke who towered above me, resplendent in the blue, damson and gold of the Tenth Hussars.

As I stood up a deep voice said to me:

'We are very pleased. We think everything is very, very pretty.' It was the voice of Queen Mary.

Queen Mary's wonderfully *soignée* appearance on all occasions is now part of social history. I have never revealed that at one time I was honoured by a command to design gowns for Her Majesty.

One day, shortly before the war, Miss Weller, Queen Mary's devoted dresser, telephoned me to say that she had been requested to pay a visit to Bruton Street to see my collection with the intention of selecting some gowns.

Miss Weller came, reviewed the dresses and decided upon one particular model as being suitable. It was a sheath-like affair of glittering soft green mother-of-pearl, called 'Fish Out of Water'.

The mannequin who wore the dress was Fritzi, that flat-figured girl of brunette beauty, but I could not imagine how the dress could possibly transform itself suitably to become the *grande dame* figure of the Queen. Miss Weller insisted that after a few adroit adjustments it would be all right, and then selected a sample in a lovely shade of aquamarine blue, to be embroidered with aquamarine sparkles and sent to Marlborough House.

'Her Majesty desires you to make three dresses, Mr Hartnell,' said Miss Weller. 'Perhaps one of silver brocade and possibly one of mauve lace.'

It was arranged that I should submit watercolour sketches of the silver and mauve dresses and, with a loyal heart, I sat down and drew the two designs.

I found no difficulty in the drawing and painting of the sketches, but I was somewhat embarrassed concerning the question of the delineation of Queen Mary's well-known head and figure. You see, to draw the wearer of a type obviously differing from that of a Royal client is stupid, and on the other hand to attempt to do an actual likeness (apart from being difficult to do in the space of about that of a postage stamp) is most definitely not desired. A medium likeness must therefore be employed, so as not to give offence in either direction.

Luckily, my pencil and paintbrush achieved a method of representation which apparently occasioned no offence; and I still have those sketches.

The morning following the delivery of my sketches a Lady-in-Waiting telephoned. 'Her Majesty approves of all the three sketches you sent—but I am commanded to inform you that your estimate of 35 guineas for the blue embroidered dress does not meet with the Queen's approval.'

'Please …' I started to stammer, as my heart's hopes drained through the soles of my shoes.

'No,' continued the voice, overwhelming my awkward interruption. 'Her Majesty desires me to say that the price of 35 guineas for the dress is much too little. Her Majesty desires to pay 45 guineas for the dress, and the same amount for the other dresses, the designs of which Her Majesty finds perfectly beautiful.'

Barely three months after the wedding of the Duke and Duchess of Gloucester, I was to see the Duchess of York again, but now under the shadow of national bereavement, for in January of 1936 King George V had died at Sandringham. I went to 145 Piccadilly, the London home of His Royal Highness the Duke of York, to discuss and quickly provide a few black dresses for the Duchess for the Court mourning period.

On reflection I think Her Royal Highness wished, with her true feminine intelligence, to know more fully the professional capacity of my dressmakers. Having assured herself on this point, it might then be easier to divide her patronage between my own house and that of Madame Handley Seymour.

I remember that fine mansion in Piccadilly which was totally destroyed during the war, and recall seeing Princess Elizabeth and her sister playing happily together in the garden. My sketches seemed to have pleased the Duchess. They have been borrowed by Mr James Laver and are now in the archives of the Victoria and Albert Museum.

That year, 1936, was one of suspense, with a growing unease about the Coronation. Would our new Sovereign be crowned as a bachelor? The Coronation day had been fixed for May 1937, and as far as I recall few plans were made in advance. I think people were already feeling the strain of international affairs. There was war in Spain, Hitler in Germany, and trouble in Abyssinia. All these things had an indirect effect upon every branch of the luxury trades, and dressmaking is a most fragile flowering. At the end of the year came the drama of the Abdication, followed almost at once by a headlong rush to get everything ready for the new Coronation in May.

Early in 1937 I was summoned to Buckingham Palace and told to consider the dresses to be worn by the Maids of Honour who would attend Her Majesty. The expert Madame Handley Seymour had been entrusted to make the Coronation dress for the new Queen.

It was to be the first of countless visits to that vast building to which the Royal Family had transferred itself from 145 Piccadilly. For me it was an entirely new world in atmosphere, but not in the least terrifying. I was, and still am, particularly happy whenever I put my first step into this magnificent Palace. One becomes immediately aware of a sense of well-ordered calm, kindliness and courtesy which permeates down through every member of the staff of the Royal household.

Both the King and the Queen had been studying the historic picture of the Coronation of Queen Victoria painted by Sir George Hayter, and had been impressed by the charming appearance of the Maids of Honour. Their Majesties pointed out the head-wreaths of gilded wheat which the trainbearers wore. Using this as the *leit-motif* of the accompanying dress, I drew a design of stiff ivory satin with a high corsage and short sleeves, the dress embroidered with a wheat-ear motif in pearls, crystal and gold.

Before I retired from Buckingham Palace that afternoon the King invited me to inspect some of the decorative pictures which portrayed many beautiful dresses of the Victorian period. Cigarette in hand, he led me off to one of the picture galleries and many other of the State Apartments to view the paintings by Winterhalter who endowed his women, particularly the lovely Empress Eugenie of France, and the yet more lovely Empress Elizabeth of Austria, with such regal and elegant grace and truly captured the very spirit of the mid-century decades. His Majesty made it clear in his quiet way that I should attempt to capture this picturesque grace in the dresses I was to design for the Queen. Thus it is to the King and Winterhalter that are owed the fine praises I later received for the regal renaissance of the romantic crinoline. As I withdrew, the King told me to return with my sketchbook and pencil if there were any details I had forgotten. Fortunately, I have a photographic mind for dress but it was the first of many occasions on which I discovered the King's practical kindness.

Among the many events jostling each other in the months before the Coronation were State Visits from the King of the Belgians and the King of Rumania. I was invited to submit sketches for the Queen's dresses at each banquet.

For the State Banquet in honour of the Belgian monarch, I made a *robe de style* of gleaming silver tissue over hooped *carcasse* of stiffened silver gauze, with a deep *berthe* collar of silver lace encrusted with glittering diamonds. Across this flux of silver the Queen wore the bright blue riband of the Order of the Garter pinned by a diamond star. This was the first great dress I designed for any member of the Royal Family.

In honour of the visit of King Carol of Romania I provided a dress of pearl grey satin, *bouffant* and trailing, embroidered with grey pearls, silver and amethyst. This dress was never worn. For, on the morning of the day of the banquet, there appeared in a newspaper a detailed description, though with no mention of the designer's name, of this important dress. His Majesty was most displeased and the dress abandoned.

Although innocent of offence, I had to make deep apology and can only think that some over-zealous member of my staff must have let slip, or given away, the news of the dress before it was delivered to the Palace.

I must, however, have been forgiven for I was not stopped in my task of preparing the dresses for the Maids of Honour. And, furthermore, Her Royal Highness the Duchess of Gloucester also commissioned me to make her dress for the Coronation.

About this time I received from Marlborough House a command to make some dresses for Her Majesty Queen Mary. The fittings for the day were over and, as I left, Queen Mary said:

'Mr Hartnell, I suppose you have visited the exhibition at the Royal School of Needlework to see the Coronation dresses on display?'

I explained that, in my eagerness to do so, I had twice travelled up to Kensington only to find an endless queue of waiting spectators and had been obliged to return disappointed.

'What a pity,' was all Queen Mary said, as I bowed myself out.

The next day I received a card of invitation to the Needlework Exhibition. Across the top was written 'Kindly allow Mr Hartnell to view the Exhibition without delay', and the signature was 'Mary R'.

Early in the following year came another summons from Buckingham Palace that proved to be an exceptional test of ingenuity and improvisation. The Queen told me of the coming State Visit to France, the first big event of the new reign, and I was asked to make Her Majesty's dresses.

A Royal trousseau for a Queen to wear in Paris conjured up visions of most romantic fancy and I came away from the Palace that morning in a mood of exultation. I hurried down to the country in order to start without disturbance the task of designing some thirty dresses, grand dresses to be worn from morning to midnight under the most critical eyes in the world, and I thought back grimly to my first painful assault on Paris.

Naturally, I had in mind a repetition of the theme of the crinoline dresses which I had made a year before for the visits of the Kings of Belgium and Romania, but first I had to visualize the stage on which the Queen would be the principal figure.

Unusual and light clear tones are the favourite colours for ladies of the Royal Family, for they must stand out, yet be distinguishable in a subtle and dignified way. The Paris *mise en scène* offered special problems. What would be the colour background? What, for example, were the strident colours in the uniforms of the Garde Republicaine and the romantic Spahis? What would be the most vivid colours at the great public ceremonies?

This was my first encounter with the dress problem presented by the strong colour of the Grand Cordon of the Legion of Honour—a kind of biting, sealing-wax red—which Her Majesty would be wearing in the French capital.

The King and Queen were to be in Paris for about four days and the wardrobe had to be designed for some five banquets, for State receptions, garden parties, processional drives, and an attendance at a Grand Gala of the Opera.

I submitted my designs, which were graciously accepted. Work on the dresses went smoothly and by June we visited the Palace for the first fittings. Then grief came to the Queen. Barely three weeks before she was due to leave for France, Her Majesty's mother, the Countess of Strathmore, died, and the Court went into mourning. In Paris the President at once called a halt to the preparations for the welcome.

But the Queen was the first to realize that there could scarcely be a cancellation of a State Visit so far advanced, only a postponement. After the first shock of her bereavement she faced the problem of her dress. Could she possibly visit the gay city of Paris in mid-summer and for such a festive occasion, dressed in deep mourning? As a nation the French might have a taste for heavy and excessive black, but would they appreciate it on an occasion designed as happy evidence of an *entente* in an already troubled Europe?

I was again summoned to the Palace where some preliminary discussion took place on how far the work on the wardrobe had gone. It had, of course, been made in many lovely colourings which were now unwearable. I ventured my own solution of the problem.

'Is not white a Royal prerogative for mourning, Your Majesty?' I suggested.

Purple is the usual colour associated with Royalty at such times as these, but there are precedents for white and it was settled that I was to pass, as it were, a magic wand over the whole collection and transform all the dresses into white in the fortnight that was left to us; for the visit had merely been postponed two weeks to the latter part of July.

Although it was a gigantic task in the little remaining time, from a dressmaker's point of view white is much easier to handle, as there is no matching of materials required and no special dyeing to cause delays. Silks, satins, velvet, cloth, taffeta, tulle, chiffon and lace were all to be in white.

The five all-white dresses for the principal occasions stand out in my memory. One for the evening reception at the Elysée Palace had its bodice and billowing skirt composed of hundreds of yards of narrow Valenciennes lace, sprinkled with silver. For the Gala at the Opera Her Majesty wore a spreading gown of thick white satin, the skirt draped with festoons of satin, held by clusters of white camellias. The Queen wore a dress that trailed on the green grass of the lawns at the Garden Party at Bagatelle. It was of the finest cobweb lace and tulle and with it was worn a sweeping hat delicately bordered with white osprey.

It was while watching the ballet, performed by the lakeside on the Ile Enchanté, that the Queen opened a parasol of transparent lace and tulle and delighted all the onlookers. At a stroke, she resuscitated the art of the parasol makers of Paris and London.

A magnificent luncheon was held in the Galeries des Glaces at the Palace of Versailles where the Queen appeared in a spreading dress, again of ground length, in white organdie, embroidered all over in openwork design of *broderie anglaise*. The white leghorn hat was softly trimmed with a ribbon of dense black velvet.

Before leaving Paris, Her Majesty laid a wreath on the newly-opened War Memorial at Villers Bretonneux Amiens. She wore for that occasion a simple *ensemble* of white crêpe and a hat of white wings.

Paris never looked so beautiful to me as in those few days of July 1938. I recall the night of the Gala at the Opera, when many thousands of Parisians in the streets would not go home and a morning paper proclaimed: 'Today France is a Monarchy again. We have taken the Queen to our hearts. She rules over two nations.

On the last day of the visit I was in the Ritz Hotel bar, sipping a champagne cocktail in the early evening when I heard a *chasseur* from the telephone booth crying, 'Monsieur 'Artnell! Monsieur 'Artnell!'

I was, of course, on call at any hour of the day or night during the visit, and had to leave my name from place to place wherever I went.

It was, I found, a message from the Countess Spencer, one of Her Majesty's Ladies-in-Waiting.

'Can you come along to the Quai d'Orsay to see their Majesties at about seven o'clock?' she asked.

I hurried back to my hotel and changed into white tie and tailed coat and wondered whether something had gone wrong, after all.

With my *laissez passer*, my taxi was allowed to go through the approaches to the Quai d'Orsay, across the bridge and stop at the entrance of the residential wing of the lovely building in which the

King and Queen were guests of the French Republic. Then up the stairs, through the big doors, along passages and more stairs, passing from one uniformed *huissier* to another, until I finally arrived at the Royal apartments.

Here I was received by the Duchess of Northumberland, the Mistress of the Robes, who was dressed in a white evening dress of lily-like beauty that perfectly suited her slender height. She wore among her jewels a most magnificent kind of stomacher or pendulous corsage ornament of inch square emeralds.

A door of a small room was opened and there stood the King and Queen. It was a wonderful sight; a unity of white, scarlet and gold. The King was in his Field Marshal's full uniform of scarlet and gold and his Orders glittered under the candelabra. The Queen was wearing her white, gold and silver crinoline dress, with the vermilion sash of the Legion of Honour.

Her Majesty generously said that it was good of me to come and she wished me to know how pleased they were with the dresses. I made a second bow.

Their Majesties were about to leave for the reception at the Elysée Palace, the President's house, and the grand staircase was already lined with men of the magnificent Garde Républicaine.

'Please have a glass of champagne before you leave,' said the Queen as she prepared to depart.

'It is very good champagne, I can assure you,' added His Majesty with a smile, as he turned to go.

After the departure of their Majesties I stayed a few days longer in Paris and began to forget the bitterness of my first visit in the more than generous praise that was now accorded my all-white *ensemble* for the Queen. I was made an *Officier d'Académie* and, equally gratifying, received warm congratulations from the critical French dressmakers themselves. It is not the only time that they have made generous comment. Not long ago, Christian Dior showed his exquisite collection at the Savoy Hotel. He invited me as Chairman of the Incorporated Society of London Fashion Designers.

'Whenever I try to think of something particularly beautiful,' said M. Dior to the guests and journalists present, 'I think always of those lovely dresses that Mr Hartnell made for your beautiful Queen when she visited Paris.'

Soon I was commanded to provide the Queen's wardrobe for the State Visit to Canada and the United States of America in the spring and summer of 1939. This time I was not controlled in design by white monotone, but there were other problems including what may be called 'dress diplomacy'. This is, of course, a development that has come with the rapid communications of our modern world, including the transfer of photographs by air and radio. The psychology of a vast public that may not always see the Queen in person has to be taken into account.

For instance, should Her Majesty wear a magnificent dress of white satin and turquoise in Ottawa, she would not appear, even for an exactly similar occasion, in that same outfit in Montreal. The people of Montreal would expect a new and different dress and might consider it a slight if the Queen wore the Ottawa dress which they would have seen in their morning newspapers. So the task for the designer of a wardrobe for a State Visit is indeed a responsible one.

For this prolonged tour I was most considerately given, from Buckingham Palace, a complete and detailed itinerary. For each day there would be six or seven occasions demanding a change of costume.

In one instance a suitable dress was needed for the Queen, while travelling by train, to awake and dress into at four o'clock in the morning when the Royal train paused at some railway station. Her Majesty was expected, with the King, to meet and greet the loyal people ranged alongside the platform. Should this be a grand dress as worn at midnight, or a little dress for breakfast? A compromise was found. It was a kind of 'hostess dress', as they are known in the United States, a long flowing *négligée* dress in nectarine velvet touched with a narrow band of sable.

Dresses had also to be suitable for every extreme of climate, from the sultry streets of New York in a heat wave, through the damp heat of a garden party at the White House, right up to the icy heights of the Rocky Mountains.

Overcoats were, with difficulty, designed to harmonize with gum boots. In contrast handles of diamonds and sapphires—gifts from Indian Rajahs—were fastened to delicate parasols of the flimsiest champagne lace.

Another important consideration was the packing of all these clothes together with their hats and all other accessories for the long and restrictive journeys. The personal maid is required to pack only those which are necessary to be worn in or leaving the train, while all the other dress luggage is sent on ahead to the city where the next public functions are to take place.

Soon after Her Majesty's return to London, in the summer of 1939, I was called to the Palace. The Queen opened a small drawer of her dressing table, and handed me a charming little jewel box of carnation pink leather that contained a set of golden cuff links with the crimson and blue enamelled initials, 'E.R.'

Three weeks later war was declared and I reported to the War Office. I was informed that, as the war would probably last six months, my services were not likely to be required. Besides, I was told that I was too old for the fighting services. Eventually I joined the Home Guard.

— CHAPTER TEN —

I might, perhaps, have been useful to the War Office in camouflage work, for I had had many years of experience in the very antithesis of the art. It had been my special task to make figures stand out in sharp relief to background, as has to be done in the case of Royalty. One of the essential elements of a majestic wardrobe is visibility. As a rule, ladies of the Royal Family wear light coloured clothes because such colours are more discernible against a great crowd, most of which will be wearing dark everyday colours.

Royalty usually travels at a slow pace (whether in an open car or a closed carriage) out of consideration for the onlookers. When only the head and shoulders of the occupant can be seen, clear and lovely colours are chosen. A similar technique is adopted in many a great stage production when the other players arid the *corps de ballet*, clothed in colours strong or dark, become a subdued background to the floodlit appearance of the leading figure in silver, gold, white or pastel.

The war brought a new dress problem to the Queen. What could she wear when visiting bombed sites and the devastated areas all over the country? How should she appear before the distressed women and children whose own kingdoms, their small homes, had been shattered and lay crumbled at her feet?

In black? Black does not appear in the rainbow of hope. Conscious of tradition, the Queen made a wise decision in adhering to the gentle colours, and even though they became muted into what one might call dusty pink, dusty blue and dusty lilac, she never wore green and she never wore black. She wished to convey the most comforting, encouraging and sympathetic note possible; and the world knows how well she succeeded.

One further point in this matter of visibility; it is also a part of tradition that all the hats worn by the Royal ladies must turn up and away from the brow, or at least reveal the face. The hats made for Her Majesty by Mr Aage Thaarup were always innocent of veils.

Many ordinary women, in times of personal distress, find comfort behind sheltering veils, but to the women of whom I write, except at a Royal funeral, they are not acceptable.

During the war the Government had meanwhile introduced a system of strict control known as 'austerity' dressing. To these limitations in dress, which stipulated how much material, how many seams a dress could comprise, how much adornment and how wide the collar or belt of a dress might be, the Queen adhered strictly.

For some vital Diplomatic soirees, however, an impressive dress was needed and, in lieu of forbidden embroideries, I painted by hand garlands of wax-like lilac and glossy green leaves on a voluminous gown of white satin, with which Her Majesty wore ornaments of diamonds and rubies. Dresses from the erstwhile peaceful years were retinted and rearranged.

The Government further introduced a 'utility' style. Specially low-priced materials were manufactured, still controlled by limitation of quantity, to be used for these clothes which were made available to the public at modest and regulated selling prices. Early in this period I received a telephone call from a firm of wholesale dressmakers who asked if I would consider designing utility wear. I declined this unusual offer but later I was urged by the Board of Trade to consider it favourably. It was explained that my name, used as designer of these clothes, would help to popularize them in the eyes of the women of this country.

But I held a Warrant as Dressmaker 'By Appointment' to Her Majesty the Queen and feared that the designing of purposefully cheap dresses might not harmonize with that status. In doubt, I laid this question before the Queen herself.

'You have made so many charming things for me,' she counselled, 'that if you can do likewise for my countrywomen, I think it would be an excellent thing to do.'

I acted on this advice and my name became linked with the utility clothes. Instead of designing lavish dresses, regardless of expense, it was suddenly my duty to study every eighth of a yard of material, every button and every buttonhole in the production of these utility dresses. As a result of this collaboration hundreds of thousands of dresses have been manufactured for the home and export markets.

Another of my occupations was to design and paint patterns for the printed materials made by The Calico Printers Association of Manchester. This firm was cut off from its co-operation with its French designers; so, with the help of the delightful Princess Galitzine, we produced home printed materials which were exported, literally by the mile, to many parts of the world.

People engaged in manufacturing textiles and the business of making dresses occupied a dual position in those war years. As far as exports were concerned we were very important; but, on the home front, clothing manufacturers became servants of the Board of Trade.

One interesting venture which took place during the war was sponsored by the Board of Trade under the kindly guidance of the late Marquess and present Dowager Marchioness of Willingdon. It was an essay in the art of export-cum-propaganda and resulted in the sending to South America of a group of mannequins dressed by all the leading London houses.

Her Excellency Dona Isabel Moniz de Aragao, wife of His Excellency the Brazilian Ambassador to the Court of St James's, was more than pleased with the result of the visit of the English dresses to South America. She suggested I should infuse some of the characteristics of the Latin-American costumes into the modern dresses of my London collection.

Although a delightful and tempting idea, I was bound to explain to Her Excellency that war-time restrictions prohibited such a project. However, after some lively discussions at the beautiful Brazilian Embassy in Mount Street, I agreed to re-create, in miniature, all the authentic costumes of the twenty Latin-American countries, and give an exhibition of these costumes, on figurines, with the dual object of bringing to the notice of Great Britain the beauty of the Latin-Americas and, at the same time, devoting the exhibition to the cause of that great charity, the Soldiers' Sailors' and Airmen's Families Association.

A committee for the exhibition was inaugurated with Marie,

Marchioness of Willingdon, C.I., CBE, as President, myself as Chairman, and my attractive and indefatigable secretary, Ann Price, as the Committee's secretary; and their acceptance to be Vice-Presidents was received from all the Ambassadors, Ministers and Charges d'Affaires of the entire twenty countries.

A special Selection Committee was also formed, including the Marchioness of Donegall, the Baroness Ravensdale, Lady Juliet Duff, Lady Clare Hartnell—my distant cousin by marriage—with Sir Shane Leslie and Mr James Laver.

The task of finding, depicting and deciding upon the authentic costumes of these countries was a task both onerous and delicate. For one thing, the smaller countries did not boast a national costume, and secondly it appeared that in some cases the most beautiful costume was that favoured by the lighter ladies of a country. It was imperative that I should present only those dresses as were worn by the great ladies of highest Latin-American social standing.

Meanwhile, I had to cut out twenty torso shapes of canvas, which were then soundly stuffed and impaled upon small bamboo supports. When the heads arrived in white plaster, I painted them all in warm skin colourings and dabbed their lips and finger tips with crimson nail varnish.

Among many distinguished assistants, including all the Ambassadors and their families, Bernard Tussaud supplied me with a special rouge for the high-moulded cheek bones, and Madame Gustave, the famous perruquier, made twenty exquisite little wigs in varying coiffures.

War shortages caused some difficulty in the construction and erection of the exhibition. No wood was permissible or obtainable so I smashed down a small partition in my kitchen to make the wooden struts across which was stretched workmanlike Hessian to provide the plinths.

Rich materials were unobtainable, with or even without coupons, so my patchwork quilts were unpicked and the pieces mingled with any pre-war remnants and patterns from my workrooms.

When all was at last ready, the exhibition was officially opened in October, 1944, and honoured by the presence of Her Majesty the

Queen, now the Queen Mother. I conducted Her Majesty around the room, explaining each costume in turn. When we looked at the figure of Nicaragua, a simple peasant costume in a small printed brocade of cherry and white, I explained that in order to express the simplicity of this character I had merely used an old piece of stuff of somewhat ordinary quality, so as to express the unobtrusive character of the peasant-like figure.

'Indeed!' observed Her Majesty serenely. 'I see you used a piece of my last year's evening wrap to do so.'

Later, the Association and I were honoured by visits from both Their Royal Highnesses the Duchess of Gloucester and the Duchess of Kent. The Duchess of Gloucester admired the Bolivian horse-woman and her fine little leather saddle. I did not tell her the story behind the smart little character, the nobleman's daughter who sent to England for a certain Captain Dashforth to look after her string of beautiful horses. After a while, she discovered his infidelities and he was seen no more.

Another English cavalier was sent for, a Captain Dashett. Riding along one day together, he asked the senorita what had happened to his great friend who had visited this country a year or so before. The senorita reined in her horse, blew a perfect ring from a little cigar and said casually, 'You are sitting on his skin.'

Later, the exhibition of Latin-American costumes went on tour, visiting most of the big cities of Great Britain. In Bristol on 1st May, 1945, Her Majesty Queen Mary graciously paid a visit and particularly admired the figure of Cuba, the Pearl of the Antilles, dressed as a bride and finely embroidered with seed pearls.

A lovely figure robed entirely in aquamarine blue, Queen Mary stood erect as she signed the visitors book.

'Gee!' exclaimed a young American officer. 'I'll tell my women-folk back home that, in England, ladies stand up to write and do it without glasses; and a British grandmother, too, apart from being a real Queen.'

These twenty pretty little figurines are still stored safely away in their packing cases and Mr James Laver has kindly given them sanctuary in the Victoria and Albert Museum. They did their duty by strengthening the understanding between this country and the Latin-Americas. The little ambassadresses of fashion also earned the splendid sum of £10,000 for the families of our soldiers, sailors and airmen.

The visit to South America was an undoubted success, and brought acclaim to British dressmakers, but there was another development, to me of almost equal importance. It brought together amicably designers who had hitherto regarded one another with some jealousy and suspicion. Now, at last, we had forgotten personal issues and, between us, we had put London in the world of international fashion.

Over the years, I had been watching the growth of a new school of English fashion. Although we were rivals, there seemed no good reason why we should not achieve a unity which might help us with the authorities. We might even gain world-wide recognition for clothes based on a native style and dignity.

So, with some misgiving, I approached Colonel Pay, the Managing Director of Worth, and then my fellow designers, urging that as we all had to deal with the same power, the Board of Trade, we might perhaps achieve more by presenting a common front. After all, in the recent tour, we had shown ourselves capable of intelligent co-operation.

So, under the urge of war-time conditions, the Incorporated Society of London Fashion Designers came into being. Of course, thanks to the happy phrase-making of the Press, we have become variously the Top Ten, the First Eleven, or the Dressmaker's Dozen, according to the membership of the moment!

Our first President was the chic Mrs Reggie Fellowes, and charming Mrs Ashley Havinden most capably took the chair. She was followed by Captain Molyneux, who, since the fall of France, had made his headquarters in London; and later by myself. The second Viscountess Rothermere followed the Hon. Mrs Fellowes; Lady Clark, wife of Sir Kenneth Clark, then became President, and this position has recently been accepted by the brilliant young Lady Pamela Berry.

I believe that the Incorporated Society of London Fashion

Designers has given the home product a stability and elegance which hitherto was possessed by Paris alone. But in our early days serious practical problems had to be faced, and one of the first was for the uniform of the Women's Royal Army Corps hitherto known as the ATS. Three members of the Incorporated Society—Creed, Molyneux and myself—were officially requested to submit designs for the new uniform.

It was suggested that the workmanlike and military khaki might be replaced for the walking-out dress. I turned over in my mind the value of such staunch colours as deep burgundy, dull chocolate brown, slate grey or a becoming bottle green. Blue, either in navy or any shade of grey-blue, was impossible, for they were severally already in use for the uniforms of the WRNS and the WRAF. The range of colour was therefore limited.

I had no idea of the conceptions of Creed and Molyneux, nor was it advisable that we should compare notes on this subject, for a designer should have independence to produce variety of design and style.

For military and technical advice I was fortunate in being able to consult the capable and delightful Dame Mary Tyrwhitt, then acting head of the Women's Corps. The formation of the tunic and the cutting of the skirt was left entirely to my tailors and myself. Dame Mary urged me to remember, however, that I was not now dressing some thousand mannequins, perfect in face and figure— although a few might be found in her ranks. I was to produce a costume that would have to be worn by many women of more than mature proportions and rarely of willowy height. The uniform must be adaptable to all these different figures and still look becoming.

I tackled the skirt first, for that is the most difficult. It could not be too straight or tight-fitting to encumber the young lady whilst scrambling into Army lorries, or mounting civilian omnibuses. Neither could it be full-swinging, not because of the flirtatious breezes of Salisbury Plain, but because too generous a use of material would add to the cost. A simple skirt, with four seams, was finally produced with two panels cut on the straight and the two side panels on the cross.

For the tunic I borrowed an idea from the Hussars. Three inserted and fitted bands, in diminishing size, started broadly across the bust and narrowed to the waist. It was neatly belted and no button was to appear below the belt, as this is inclined to accentuate a slight 'tummy'.

I had drawn all my designs in the deep bottle green colour, imagining this to be a good background for brass buttons and a foil to the black or brown leather accessories of shoes and gloves. As a touch of contrasting colour I added a band of light tan brown around the hat, on the shoulder straps and finally as a sash, borrowed from the tunics of some Guards' regiments, around the waist.

When all was finished the design had to be reviewed by high-ranking officers of the WRAC, before being finally submitted to His Majesty the King. Much to my surprise, I was then told that my design, if accepted, would be used also for the uniforms of the Queen Alexandra's Royal Army Nursing Corps on the understanding that the colour combination would be changed to that already worn by the nurses, steel grey and scarlet.

It is pleasant to recall that His Majesty chose the uniform of my designing, although no individual designer's name was revealed at the time. It was then my privilege immediately to make the first uniform for the Colonel-in-Chief of the WRAC, Her Royal Highness the Princess Royal. I was also fortunate enough to make acceptable designs for the women who did such magnificent service in the British Red Cross Society. The request for these came in the form of a charming letter from the Countess of Limerick, Vice-Chairman of the Society, and with her help and that of the Viscountess Falmouth, Deputy Chairman, I evolved the new and more practical design in both red cloth and blue canton. With it, of course, would be worn the apron, neatly belted and bearing a significant Red Cross in vivid scarlet upon the bosom of pure white linen.

But this varied work, undertaken often at short notice, and in addition to the general strain of war-time London, resulted in a breakdown of my health. Fortunately for me my business manager, Captain Mitchison, had recently returned from war service in South East Asia and agreed to accompany me on what sounded like a most invigorating business trip to South America.

— CHAPTER ELEVEN —

The Latin-American Exhibition had aroused so much interest that Dona Isabel Moniz de Aragao suggested I should take a collection of my own modern dresses to Rio de Janeiro. This was warmly seconded by my friend, Captain Andrew Duncan, a member of the British Diplomatic Mission in Brazil. I agreed to go and invited Robert Nesbitt to join me with his beautiful newly-married wife, Iris, who would act as *mannequin-mondaine*.

Lights glittered in the three great bays of Rio as the aeroplane landed on the airfield, not in glorious sunshine but more like Ilkley Moor or Clapham Common in a rainstorm.

Captain Duncan conducted us to the Copacabana, that gleaming white and palatial hotel which dominates the social life of this wealthy and fabulous city. We were entertained by the rich set of Rio, for there is no other set! After the *grafinos*, no middle class exists, only the city workers.

Most diplomatically, Captain Duncan reserved one lengthy table at which sat a carefully chosen representation of the elite of Rio de Janeiro, seated with the strictest observance of protocol. They were:

His Imperial Highness Prince Pedro de Orleans et Braganga.

Her Imperial Highness Princesse Esperanza de Orleans et Braganca.

Princesse Theresa de Orleans et Braganca.

His Excellency The British Ambassador and Lady St Clair Gainer.

The Swedish Minister and Madame Ragnar Kumlin.

The Marquess and Marchioness of Linlithgow.

The Ambassador Joachim de Souza Leao.

As I conducted Mrs Nesbitt from the supper guests to take part in the mannequin parade, the ladies and gentlemen of Brazil raised horrified eyebrows. Apparently, the mannequins of that country do not mingle in social circles, and it took Lady Linlithgow a long time to calm their ruffled feathers and explain that in our country young ladies of the best social strata take part in the display of dress. But the Brazilian ladies were soon enraptured and, within a few days, the entire collection, with the exception of the wedding dress, was sold.

At one elegant reception was Madame Lupescu, the constant companion of ex-King Carol of Romania. They occupied the entire top floor of the Copacabana Hotel and resided there *en prince*, surrounded by a small court of faithful retainers.

Lupescu was a most striking woman with orange hair and a flamboyant autumnal beauty. It was explained to her with regret that the only remaining model was the wedding dress, a wraith-like affair of flimsy silver gauze, falling softly as drapery around a Greek statue. Later Madame Lupescu bought this silver dress through Madame Zulnie-David, the best-known *couturière* in Brazil who was generously housing my collection.

Some while later Lupescu, fearing that her end was near, donned the bridal gown and lay on her death bed in it, surrounded by candles and lilies. As the candles burned low, King Carol pronounced her his Queen. Soon afterwards, Madame Lupescu stirred in her silver shroud, my wedding dress, and recovered.

From Buenos Aires in the adjoining Argentine came Oliver Blackler, the representative from the Argentine firm of Harrods in Buenos Aires. His directors, he explained, would like me to show my collection there. I explained that the entire collection was sold, but if he would place at my disposal a large workroom of girls, directed by a capable French fitter, I would buy the necessary materials from Harrods, bring my paintbox and sketch block with me and design and make a collection for them on the spot. It was arranged and we all migrated to the Argentine. With the aid of a Franco-Anglo-Espano interpreter, I had the collection of 100 dresses ready within two weeks.

In Buenos Aires I met the attractive and wealthy Madame Alberto Dodero, formerly Betty Sudmark of London, who was styled the Lady-in-Waiting to Senora Eva Peron. She kindly arranged a meeting between us and, in her private apartment, I was presented to this lady, once of the people, but now in high authority as the brilliant and influential wife of the dictator of Argentina.

Her beauty then was remarkable. She had an ivory complexion that shone as though polished in the fashion of some Spanish beauties, fine dark eyes and carefully coiffured hair, the colour of golden syrup.

I hurried back to tell the directors of Harrods the exciting news that Madame Peron would attend my dress show. The result was unexpected. The agitated directors were unanimous in upbraiding me for interfering with the arrangements. They predicted a social calamity. The presence of Madame Peron would cause all the other great ladies to make their instant and disdainful departure. But by now it was too late to retract my *faux pas*.

With the entrance of Madame Peron, the entire working staff abandoned their posts of duty. They flocked to the pavement or stood in crowded ranks around all the departments and floors through which their heroine would pass.

'*Viva Evita!*' they shouted.

Triumphantly she made her way through the frenzied and cheering mob, until the directors and I greeted her as she entered the seething tea room at Harrods, where so many plots have been hatched, revolutions fomented and Governments overthrown.

The great ladies had come but, as Eva Peron entered, not one of them moved, though all heads were turned towards her. With a calm and isolated assurance she reviewed the entire lengthy collection. Afterwards she chose for herself two black and jet embroidered dresses. My great disappointment was that every man and woman in that vast crowd gazed steadily at her throughout the lengthy proceedings.

Nobody looked at my dresses. Eva had killed the show.

— CHAPTER TWELVE —

During the war I had lived in a small Nash-designed villa, the Tower House, in Regent's Park, but on returning to England from South America, I went to live again in my house in the cool glades of Windsor Forest. I was restored to health by the sunshine and eager to resume work. The opportunity was not long in coming.

Early in July, 1947, the engagement had been announced of Her Royal Highness Princess Elizabeth to Lieutenant Philip Mountbatten RN. The wedding would take place on 20th November and I was delighted to be summoned to Buckingham Palace to discuss her dresses with the Queen who asked me also to submit some sketches for the Princess's wedding gown. In the middle of August I heard the great news that a design of mine had been approved.

This gave me less than three months to complete the dress and train. It also made it necessary for me to cancel a proposed visit to Dallas, Texas, where, with Christian Dior, I was to receive the coveted Neiman-Marcus award for contemporary influence on fashion, a kind of dressmaker's 'Oscar'. But I also wanted to bring back great quantities of small white American pearls for I was already visualizing a bridal gown of fine pearl embroidery. Meanwhile, I roamed the London art galleries in search of classic inspiration and, fortunately, found a Botticelli figure in clinging ivory silk, trailed with jasmine, smilax, syringa and small white rose-like blossoms. I thought these flora might be interpreted on a modern dress through the medium of fine white crystals and pearls—if only I had the pearls.

A few weeks later, my manager, Captain Mitchison, returned from America and was asked at the customs if he had anything to declare. Raising the deep collar of his British warm he bent forward mysteriously and answered in lowered tone:

'Yes, ten thousand pearls, for the wedding dress of Princess Elizabeth!'

Somewhat started, the officials retained the pearls until the prescribed duty was paid, but soon the tiny American pearls were being delicately fastened by needle and thread to a glossy background of English satin.

Then came the problem of the satin. What was the nationality of the worms that had provided the silk from which the satin was made and with which I intended to make the dress? Her Majesty the Queen had expressed the wish that I should use a certain satin made at Lullington Castle which is directed by the delightful Lady Hart-Dyke. This superb satin, rich, lustrous and stiff, I was able to use for the lengthy train, but for the dress itself a slightly more supple material of similar tint was preferable. I ordered it from the Scottish firm of Wintherthur near Dunfermline; and then the trouble started. I was told in confidence that certain circles were trying to stop the use of the Scottish satin on the grounds of patriotism; the silk worms, they said, were Italian, and possibly even Japanese! Was I so guilty of treason that I would deliberately use *enemy* silk-worms?

I telephoned through to Dunfermline, begging them to ascertain the true nationality of the worms; were they Italian worms, Japanese worms, or Chinese worms?

'Our worms,' came the proud reply, 'are Chinese worms—from Nationalist China, of course.' After which we were able to get on with the real job with a much easier conscience.

To complete the bridal retinue, I was asked to provide dresses for the eight beautiful young girls of whom the bride's sister, Her Royal Highness Princess Margaret, was the leading bridesmaid. I had already enjoyed the honour of making many dresses for Princess Margaret and had always noticed with what quick decision she chose her clothes. On this occasion, however, she most unselfishly preferred to state no opinion until the design had been also submitted for the approval of all the other bridesmaids.

These dresses were finally made of ivory silk tulle with a full flowing skirt and a tulle *fichu* swathed across the shoulders and fitted corsage. On the skirts was a milky way of small star-shaped blossoms embroidered with pearl and crystal. This repeated the motif of the bridal train which, fastened to the shoulder, stretched about fifteen yards behind the Princess.

One evening, after her young assistants had gone home, Miss Flora Ballard, my head embroideress, and I laid out fifteen yards of tracing paper flat on the linoleum workroom floor. I rolled up my shirt sleeves and wore gymnasium shoes, so that I should not slip when running up and down both sides of fifteen paper yards secured by drawing pins to the shiny linoleum.

Graphite pencil in hand, I first marked out a long line from shoulder almost to the hem of the main backbone, a central line for the graduated satin syringa and orange blossoms. Similar pearl embroideries were to mark the border edges of the train. Then, crouching on my knees, I marked in the more softly curving lines of the diamond and pearl wheat ears which feathered gracefully to the base of the train.

Sitting cross-legged and suffering from a severe cold in the head, I marked in circles the rich white roses of York to be carried out in padded satin, and centred by raised strands of pearls threaded on silver wire and raised up in relief. All these motifs had to be assembled in a design proportioned like a florist's bouquet. Wherever there was space or weakness of design I drew more wheat, more leaves, more blossom of orange, syringa or jasmine.

I have many memories of the crowded weeks that followed. I had been commanded by Her Majesty the Queen to design her dress of apricot and golden brocade, gracefully draped and trailing; also by Her Majesty Queen Mary to provide her *ensemble*, a dress and coat of golden tissue embossed with sea-blue chenille, the last dress I ever had the honour of making for that great lady.

The Princess had naturally requested, like any other bride, that no details of her dress should be made public, but we had little anticipation of the world-wide curiosity which had been aroused. Surmise became wild and almost hysterical. It was rumoured that the design would be 'pirated' and put on the wholesale market to coincide with the wedding, but I had no fear of this, knowing that the principal asset of the dress was its complicated embroidery and the time and money it would take.

A neighbour of mine had an offer of a two months' tenancy of rooms overlooking my own workrooms. I am grateful that he declined. We then had the workroom windows whitewashed and curtained with thick white muslin. The tension and speculation over the dress reached such a point, that to be quite sure the secret was preserved around the clock, my manager volunteered to sleep in the next room.

About a month before the wedding I received permission to show something of the nature of the dress to a selected group of fashion writers, each of whom would be asked to sign a promise not to reveal the details until the day of the Abbey ceremony. There was a leakage in the end, but just how it came about we could never discover. The *Giornale d'Italia* published a rough picture of my sketch obtained at the second preview a week before, and this was reproduced in the New York *Daily News*. A London paper which had not signed the pledge promptly followed suit.

That eminent historian and authority on dress, Mr James Laver, called me 'no mean poet' and wrote somewhat lyrically:

'There is a poetry in dressmaking although the unfortunate dress designer has nowadays few opportunities for many flights of fancy. Even the language of clothes is in danger of being reduced to the staccato prose of telegraphese,' he wrote. 'In his design (for the wedding dress) based on delicate Botticelli curves, he has scattered over the ivory satin garlands of white York roses carried out in raised pearls, entwined with ears of corn minutely embroidered in crystal ... the result is a colour scheme—yes! a colour scheme—surprising in its range, for a whole gamut of shades and contrasts can be held within the span of colour which is itself no colour.

'Mallarmé used to say that nothing inspired him so much as a sheet of white paper, and that he hardly dared to set down upon it the sparse notes of his ethereal music. So must the white material be envisaged, and so must the designer cast upon it the indications of his harmony; the music within the silence, the *symphonie en blanc majeurs* ... the occasion demanded a poet, and Mr Hartnell has not failed to string his lyre with art and to ring in tune.'

On the eve of the wedding, hundreds of headlines informed

the world that the 'Princess gets her Bridal Gown at Palace in 4-ft Box.' What I hoped would be the most beautiful dress I had so far made now belonged to its lovely young owner. All that was left to me was to see it worn in the setting for which I had designed it. Westminster Abbey.

With the dress went, of course, a magnificent bride's bouquet. Yvonne, my devoted saleswoman, told me after the ceremony that when she reported at the Palace to dress the bride, the *toilette* was complete but the bouquet could not be found. The personal maid to Her Royal Highness had gone in advance to the Abbey to be ready there, with my two sewing women, for any needlework emergency.

Furthermore, the rest of the staff had all been given standing room in the forecourt of the Palace to see the cortege leave. The Palace was, therefore, deserted for this one unusual moment, except for the King and his daughter, the bride.

Yvonne asked if there were not a bouquet, but the Princess had no idea where it was.

The King, of course, had no knowledge of its whereabouts, so Yvonne hurried from room to room, through long deserted corridors, prying here and there and afterwards searched the huge ground floor. Finally she discovered the bouquet in one of the porters' lodges and hurried back with it to the bride.

The spectacle in the Abbey was superb; the High Altar with its gold plate and the rich glow of the candles against the heavy brocades, the Gentlemen at Arms in their scarlet tunics and with the plumes of their helmets swaying slightly as they moved with great dignity from one point to another, and finally the glorious peal of bells as the bride approached.

On this great occasion I treasure most the memory of the young bride's graceful obeisance before her parents, the King and Queen. And the smile she gave to the assembly as, in gloss of satin and shimmer of pearl, she passed serenely from Westminster Abbey.

The years that followed the war had been occupied with preparing clothes for the many Royal tours. When the King and Queen planned a visit to South Africa with the Princesses I was commanded to make three separate wardrobes for each of the Royal ladies.

Her Majesty first set foot in South Africa wearing a panelled dress of ice blue, trimmed with a soft band of ostrich feather. At the first garden party she wore a long white chiffon dress with a large hat fringed with white ostrich fronds, the latter being a compliment to this important native product.

I recall that from two similar yachting suits of white linen made for the Princesses, His Majesty insisted that the brass buttons be removed, for they were authentic naval buttons, and replaced by plain ones.

In May of 1948 Princess Elizabeth, now with her husband, the Duke of Edinburgh, visited Paris, and again I provided nearly all the clothes for Her Royal Highness. I took care that the Gala evening dresses had small sleeves or straps, either broad or narrow, on which to affix the Orders of the scarlet Legion of Honour of the blue sash of the Garter.

A year later, Princess Margaret visited Italy and I designed many simple summer suits and dresses for this lovely young Princess. There followed visits by Her Royal Highness to Holland and Sweden and again I provided a selection of clothes.

In 1950 the President of France and Madame Auriol paid an official visit to London. Madame Massigli, the chic and fascinating wife of France's Ambassador to England, has since told me of Madame Auriol's anxious telephone call to her, inquiring what length of dress Her Majesty, now the Queen Mother, would wear when meeting her at Victoria Station. Madame Auriol remembered that when Madame Lebrun, in 1938, had arrived at the Gare du Nord, wearing a short skirt, the Queen was wearing a long one. On departure, the Queen had thoughtfully selected a short one in which to bid *au revoir* at the station to the wife of the then French President only to find that Madame Lebrun, with similar good intention, had this time donned a long one.

For this French visit I was commanded to make many sumptuous dresses for the Queen and the two Princesses. Later, when the Duchess of Kent made her important journey to Malaya I made a comprehensive collection of dresses suitable for wear in the intense heat. They were dresses of the simplest design in gossamer materials such as organza and tissue paper taffetas, with vaporous evening gowns of flowered gauze and chiffon, which the Duchess enhanced with her own beauty and elegance.

In September of 1951 I made many dresses for Princess Elizabeth for her tour of Canada with the Duke of Edinburgh. This was the first occasion upon which I was asked to design clothes of a darker colour. One *ensemble* was of deep olive green velvet, another of clear slate blue, another of holly berry red cloth with a black velvet collar.

Towards the end of that year I was busily engaged on a varied wardrobe for Her Royal Highness when she and Prince Philip, with the country's blessing, set out on their visit to Australia. After only a few days it became the heartrending duty of His Royal Highness to inform his young wife of her father's death. She was, now, by the will of God, Queen Elizabeth the Second.

— CHAPTER THIRTEEN —

Plans for the Coronation were soon set into motion, and magnificently accomplished by His Grace the Duke of Norfolk. In the
autumn, I visited the Earl Marshal's Office, in Belgrave Square,
where Bluemantle, Pursuivant of Arms, explained that a new design
was required for alternative dress to be worn by Viscountesses and
Baronesses at the Coronation.

The existing habiliment of these Peeresses was a combination
of two garments, comprising a kirtle of crimson velvet, bordered
all round with a narrow edge of miniver pure, scalloped or straight
in front, or gathered back in three festoons, each tied with a bow
of golden tinsel. This kirtle is worn over the usual full Court dress,
which should be white or slightly cream-coloured, with lace, embroidery, or brocade, according to taste. Gold and silver can be used but
no colour may be introduced into it. With this is worn a mantle with
a train, called a Robe (attached to and falling from the shoulders)
also of crimson velvet and ermine.

There was considerable concern regarding the costliness of these
robes which, hitherto, it had been imperative to wear for every
Coronation ceremony in the Abbey. Bluemantle asked if I would
undertake to evolve a design of one garment to replace the two
separate ones, and thus help reduce the cost for those ladies who
might not be as wealthy as the world imagined.

The same need for economy applied to the costly metallic cor-
onet hitherto worn by Peeresses. He asked if I would design an
inexpensive and appropriate headgear, perhaps based on the design
worn by Barons before the days of Charles II and known as a Cap of
State. The Robes of State and Coronets had not been altered since
the reign of Queen Anne and for days I puzzled over the salient
points. I wished to retain the form-fitting grace of the kirtle but to
dispose of its ugly sleeves which were about nine inches long. Also,

the kirtle stopped short in a hard, clumsy line at the feet. The Robe, of course, trailed elegantly on the floor, yet the cape of white fur adjoined at the shoulder was square and stumpy.

Eliminating the less attractive aspects of both kirtle and Robe, I chose the fitted line of the former, ignoring the sleeves, and reformed the square line of the short ermine cape of the latter into a graceful curve which, standing away from the back of the wearer, covered the tops of the arms—often the most unattractive part of the female form—and met in front, where it clasped like a broad cape collar in a high-waisted princess line. It was the most generally wearable and most flattering and feminine of all the six designs I had painted. I then designed and drew thirty ideas for the Cap of State. Meanwhile, I had to search for an inexpensive red velveteen and some cheap white pelts of the humble rabbit in an effort to effect the necessary economy.

When all was ready I returned to the Earl Marshal's office where I was most courteously received by Garter King of Arms, Sir George Bellew. Of the thirty Caps of State one was unanimously preferred. Estimates of the cost, which had turned out to be surprisingly low, were submitted to Garter and Bluemantle. The selling price had been reduced from £500 to a matter of £30.

Before I left Belgrave Square I was required to undertake the task of devising some form of head covering to be worn by those ladies who would attend the Abbey ceremony wearing, perhaps, day clothes if the short-skirted fashion were permitted. For those wearing long evening dress, tiaras were advised. Garter kindly drew for me a neat little sketch of the kind of headgear he imagined would be suitable, and after some days I returned again with a few dozen more.

It was finally agreed officially that 'those ladies attending the Coronation in short evening dress must wear a head covering which must not cover the face, but should be in the form of a veil, falling from the crown or back of the head as far as the shoulders, but not lower than the waistline. Any colour excepting black can be used and should be made in a suitably light material such as tulle, chiffon, organza or lace. This can be attached by a comb, jewelled pins, flowers, or ribbon bows—but not with feathers.'

The little Cap of State, now made up in its right materials, looked gaily modern and attractive, and was described as a crimson velvet Cap enriched with narrow gold braid and bordered with a narrow strip of white fur. The Cap was made to fit the crown of the head and had to have a gold or gold-coloured tassel or other similar decoration which consisted of a knot of gold braid ending in drop pearls.

Later I was granted the honour of an audience at Buckingham Palace. Her Majesty was pleased to approve of everything submitted to her notice and I retired feeling less guilty of having interfered with fashions favoured in the reign of good Queen Anne.

— CHAPTER FOURTEEN —

One October afternoon in 1952, Her Majesty the Queen desired me to make for her the dress to be worn at her Coronation.

I can scarcely remember what I murmured in reply. In simple conversational tones the Queen went on to express her wishes. Her Majesty required that the dress should conform in line to that of her wedding dress and that the material should be white satin. It was almost exactly five years earlier that I had put the final touches to the dress which, as Princess Elizabeth, she had worn on the day of her wedding to the Duke of Edinburgh.

When my first exhilaration was over, I settled down to study exactly what history and tradition meant by a 'Coronation dress'. I visited the London Museum and the London Library and leafed through authoritative tomes.

The first Queen Elizabeth had an inborn love of splendour, and I had visions of the sort of thing I would have created if I had been a dress designer in the sixteenth century. She had worn a tiara-like headdress with flowers and jewels in her hair, a radiating and bejewelled ruff, heavy pearl ear-rings, a fur-trimmed cloak, puffings studded with more jewels, ruffles at the wrists and a fan of peacock feathers. Her skirt opened to disclose a kirtle diapered with jewels.

All this seemed a trifle ornate and I learned that the courtiers of the period were also rather gaudy fellows, wearing jackets slashed to reveal pull-outs of the wildest colours, and dripping with jewellery. I felt that the Tudors offered little help, beyond their Rose, which I certainly hoped to introduce into the Coronation dress of 1953.

Then I turned to the study of Queen Anne, who most unhappily was crippled with gout on the day of her Coronation. She wore a dress of gold tissue with a petticoat embroidered with jewels and gold lace, and a traditional mantle of crimson velvet trimmed with miniver. There was no mention of any Mistress of the Robes, which was remarkable. The first 'mistress' was actually a man and he called himself Groom of the Stole to Charles II. It was not until Queen Anne's day that the Groom became Mistress and she was none other than Lady Sarah Churchill, the wife of the Duke of Marlborough. This ambitious and dominating lady had created the title for herself and also became 'Keeper of the Privy Purse'. The role of Mistress of the Robes then disappeared until Queen Victoria came to the Throne. The pictorial evidence of the robe and dress worn by the young Queen seems a little conflicting and her own diaries were not very helpful.

'I took off my crimson robe and kirtle and put on my supertunica of cloth of gold, also in the shape of a kirtle, which was put over a singular sort of little linen gown trimmed with lace' she wrote. I guessed that the latter would be the one on exhibition in the London Museum in Kensington Palace. More valuable were the pictures of the actual Coronation scene, showing the grouping of people around the Throne, notably the trainbearers, who, according to one witness, 'made the Queen look even smaller.'

After gathering all the factual material I could, I then retired to the seclusion of Windsor Forest and there spent many days making trial sketches. My mind was teeming with heraldic and floral ideas. I thought of lilies, roses, marguerites and golden corn; I thought of altar cloths and sacred vestments; I thought of the sky, the earth, the sun, the moon, the stars and everything heavenly that might be embroidered upon a dress destined to be historic.

Altogether, I created nine differing designs which began in almost severe simplicity and proceeded towards elaboration. I liked the last one best, but naturally did not express my opinion when I submitted these paintings to Her Majesty.

The first I showed to the Queen was an extremely simple style in lustrous white satin, lightly embroidered along the edge of the bodice and around the skirt's hem in a classic Greek-key design, somewhat similar to that worn by Queen Victoria.

The second was modern line, slender and slimly fitting, embroidered in gold and bordered with the black and white ermine tails of Royal miniver.

The third was a crinoline dress of white satin and silver tissue, encrusted with silver lace and sewn with crystals and diamonds.

The fourth was emblazoned with a theme of Madonna and arum lilies tumbling with pendant pearls.

The fifth depicted what might have been a flouting of tradition, for I had introduced a note of colour in the violets of modesty expressed in *cabochon* amethysts and in the rubies of the red roses that glittered and mingled in the waving design of wheat, picked out with opals and topaz. But Her Majesty eased my uncertainty by saying that the suggestion of colour was not inadmissible.

The sixth, again of white satin, was of spreading branches of oak leaves, in a way emblematic, with knobbly acorns of silver bullion thread that dangled on small silver crystal stalks amidst the glinting leaves of golden and copper metals. This design met with gracious approval.

The seventh introduced in bold character the Tudor Rose of England, each bloom padded and puffed in gold tissue against a white gloss of satin and shadowed and surrounded by looped fringes of golden crystals.

The eighth sketch, which automatically suggested itself to me from the previous sketches with the emblem of the Tudor Rose, was composed of all the emblems of Great Britain. Therefore it included the Thistle of Scotland, the Shamrock of Ireland and the daffodil which, at that time, I thought to be the authentic national emblem of Wales. All these floral emblems, placed in proper positions of precedence on the skirt, were to be expressed in varying tones of white and silver, using small diamonds and crystals for pinpoint coruscation.

Her Majesty approved of this emblematic impression but considered that the use of all white and silver might too closely resemble her wedding gown. She liked the theme of the fifth design and suggested that I might employ the aid of colour in representing the four emblems.

I mentioned that the gown of Queen Victoria was all white, but Her Majesty pointed out that, at the time of her Coronation in 1838, Queen Victoria was only 18 years old and unmarried, whereas she herself was older and a married woman. Therefore, the restrictions imposed upon the gown of Queen Victoria did not apply to her own. I then drew a facsimile of the chosen sketch and enjoyed the pleasure, known to all artists, of painting the small rainbow touches of pastel colours into a pencilled black and white drawing.

Later, at another audience, the Queen made a wise and sovereign observation. It was, in effect, that she was unwilling to wear a gown bearing emblems of Great Britain without the emblems of all the Dominions of which she was now Queen.

I then drew and painted the ninth design which proved more complicated than I had expected. A new design had to be provided and I found it necessary to raise up the three emblems of Scotland, Ireland and Wales to the upper portion of the skirt, thus contracting the space they occupied upon the satin background, to allow for more space below, where all the combined flowers of the Commonwealth countries could be assembled in a floral garland, each flower or leaf nestling closely around the motherly English Tudor Rose, placed in the centre.

Meanwhile, to confirm the accuracy of these emblems, I again consulted that amiable authority, Garter King of Arms, at the office of the Earl Marshal. He supplied me with a particularly decorative Tudor Rose, and the Thistle and the Shamrock proved simple. I then made the mistake of asking for the daffodil of Wales.

'A daffodil!' exclaimed Garter. 'On no account will I give you a daffodil. I will give you the correct emblem of Wales, which is the Leek.'

The leek I agreed was a most admirable vegetable, full of historic significance and doubtless of health-giving properties, but scarcely noted for its beauty. Could he not possibly permit me to use the more graceful daffodil instead?

'No, Hartnell. You must have the Leek,' said Garter, adamant.

My enthusiasm blunted, I went down to Windsor, greatly depressed. The fading afternoon light showed only barren trees, a lake glum and grey, and the whole landscape wrapped in November gloom. I went out to the vegetable garden, pulled up a leek and suddenly remembered the cap badge of the Welsh Guards. Perhaps, after all, something could be done with it. In the end, by using lovely silks and sprinkling it with the dew of diamonds, we were able to transform the earthy Leek into a vision of Cinderella charm and worthy of mingling with her sisters Rose and Mimosa in a brilliant Royal Assembly, and fit to embellish the dress of a queen.

Samples of the intended floral emblems had to be submitted to Her Majesty before the final decision was made. My embroidery rooms at once began to evolve these eleven motifs and we realized finally that the only satisfactory method of interpreting all the fine flowers was to use the silken stitchery, as well as jewels, sequins and beads, so that the despised Leek proved a real inspiration after all.

An appointment was made for some members of my staff and myself to visit Sandringham House. So, on a very cold Saturday morning, we motored up to Norfolk with two car loads of people and dresses. Apart from the now completed ninth sketch and the precious emblems, we took with us a generous collection of dresses newly prepared for the spring, from which Her Majesty might be able to select dresses for her tour of Australasia in the early part of the following year. These dresses were beautifully packed by the indispensable Florrie who accompanied us this time in the additional capacity of *habilleuse*.

The atmosphere of Sandringham is about as different from that of Buckingham Palace and Windsor Castle as could possibly be imagined, and I can well understand why successive generations of the Royal Family have such a great affection for this rambling Victorian country home and its encircling pine woods.

After luncheon we staged the most informal dress show I have ever presented, for it took place in a large bedroom of old-fashioned charm. The mannequins entered through a door that led out of a capacious white bathroom. From this quaint display some dresses were chosen as the basis of the wardrobe for Australia.

It was then my duty to present to the Queen the final sketch together with the coloured emblems. Each of them had been mounted in a circular gilded wooden frame and I laid out the following emblems:

England. The Tudor Rose, embroidered in palest pink silk, pearls, gold and silver bullion and rose diamonds.

Scotland. The Thistle, embroidered in pale mauve silk and amethysts. The calyx was embroidered in reseda green silk, silver thread and diamond dewdrops.

Ireland. The Shamrock, embroidered in soft green silk, silver thread bullion and diamonds.

Wales. The Leek, embroidered in white silk and diamonds with the leaves in palest green silk.

Canada. The Maple Leaf, in green silk embroideries, bordered with gold bullion thread and veined in crystal.

Australia. The Wattle flower, in mimosa yellow blossom with the foliage in green and gold thread.

New Zealand. The Fern, in soft green silk veined with silver and crystal.

South Africa. The Protea, in shaded pink silk, each petal bordered with silver thread. The leaves of shaded green silk and embellished with rose diamonds.

India. The Lotus flower, in mother-of-pearl embroidered petals, seed pearls and diamonds.

Pakistan. Wheat, cotton and jute. The wheat was in oat-shaped diamonds and fronds of golden crystal, the jute in a spray of leaves of green silk and golden thread, and the cotton blossom with stalks of silver and leaves of green silk.

Ceylon. The Lotus flower, in opals, mother-of-pearl, diamonds and soft green silk.

Apart from the Irish Shamrock, which was judged a little too verdant in tone, the Queen was pleased to agree to the *ensemble* as my design for her Coronation Gown.

Her Majesty Queen Elizabeth The Queen Mother, who was sitting between the Queen and Her Royal Highness Princess Margaret, had been watching the display from a slender Victorian sofa at the end of an enormous bedstead. She was pleased to accept my design for her own gown which was to be of white satin bordered with gold tissue and embroidered in a feather design of crystal, gold and diamante.

Princess Margaret then graciously ordered her dress from my sketch which depicted a white satin dress embroidered in open-worked design of *broderie anglaise*, strengthened with crystal, and with marguerites and roses worked in silver thread and shimmering with pearls.

The design I submitted for Her Majesty's trainbearers was also accepted. The interest of this design was concentrated mainly on the back of the skirt. Realizing that the Maids of Honour, carrying the Queen's State Robes of Imperial velvet, would show the backs of their dresses almost more than the front as they followed her up the aisle, I had arranged for the embroideries of small golden leaves and pearl white blossom to cascade down the backs of their billowing skirts of white satin.

The Maids of Honour were to be six beautiful young women, chosen from the noblest families in the land. They were Lady Jane Vane-Tempest-Stewart, Lady Anne Coke, Lady Moyra Hamilton, Lady Mary Baillie-Hamilton, Lady Jane Heathcote Drummond Willoughby and Lady Rosemary Spencer-Churchill.

I explained to the assembled Royal ladies the predominant motifs of the dress I was designing for Her Royal Highness the Duchess of Kent and her daughter, the young Princess Alexandra, so that there should be no clash or confusion of colour in the dresses.

For the Duchess of Kent I designed a dress of white satin embroidered with perpendicular panels of golden mosaic design, and for the Princess a diaphanous garment of white lace and tulle lightly threaded with gold.

Two more gowns for the Coronation were commanded to be made by me in white and gold brocade of varying patterns for the Countess of Euston and the Countess of Leicester, Her Majesty's Ladies of the Bedchamber.

It had in truth been a crowded hour.

— CHAPTER FIFTEEN —

The spring of 1953 was the busiest season we had ever known, and the excitement of preparation ran high as the final days arrived. Many of the specially created new crimson velvet robes were being made for the Viscountesses and Baronesses, and lovely dresses for numerous Duchesses, Marchionesses and Countesses. And row upon row of the cute little Caps of State stood on their pegs in the milliners' *atelier*.

Madame Isabelle, the inspired Parisienne *première* in charge of the Coronation Gown, found technical difficulty in making the skirt, stiffened, bejewelled and weighty, swing to the right balance. On the *mannequin de bois*, or wooden model stand, it would fall sideways, so it was entirely lined or backed with cream taffeta, reinforced with three layers of horsehair crinoline, which gave it a dignified and gentle movement.

Another attractive Parisienne, Madame Emilienne, was clever, quick and resourceful, but was finding trouble with the skirt for Her Majesty the Queen Mother. The rich border of golden tissue and the jewelled feather embroideries caused the skirt to hang in limp and disappointing nuance. This skirt was, therefore, glorified into regal fullness by mounting it on an underskirt of ivory taffeta laced with bands of horsehair and further strengthened with countless strands of whalebone.

Madame Alice found no difficulty with her dresses for the Maids of Honour, and throughout this period Miss Edie Duley and her wonderful young women were in control of all the great embroideries.

The dresses for the other ladies of the Royal Family progressed satisfactorily, and all the Maids of Honour were delighted with their train-bearers' dresses. Later, I was to witness these six exquisite young women rehearse, with the Queen, the walk, the halt, the holding and folding of the State Robes. Time after time this operation was repeated and, though it seemed to me that the Maids of Honour became a little fatigued in the process, the Queen herself remained fresh and undaunted, until she was assured that she and her retinue had acquired ceremonial perfection.

Soon there came the day for the final trying-on of the gown for Her Majesty. Unknown to the Royal wearer, I had on the left-hand side of the skirt inserted amidst the cluster of shamrocks one extra little four-leaved shamrock for luck. I am not superstitious—I am on the contrary religious—but had envisaged that, while waving through the window of the Royal Coach, she could with her left hand perhaps touch this small omen of good fortune. This the Queen did as she finally tried on her sumptuous gown and gently caressed the spreading skirt.

Although it is not etiquette for me to quote the exact terms of Her Majesty's verdict, she did use the one word, 'Glorious'.

In the opinion of some, Her Majesty looked her loveliest when all the glories of her gown were covered with an overdress of white linen made for that specially sacred moment of the Anointing. This corresponded to what Queen Victoria had referred to as her 'funny little shift, bordered with lace'. No lace or embellishment was on this garment. The fine lawn had a boat-shaped neckline, from which fell a deep collar, hiding the short jewelled sleeves, and this was hand-tucked on the cross in graduating sizes. The skirt fell from the Queen's slender waist in voluminous panels of sunray pleating and fastened in the small of the back in the becoming line of an apron.

The fastening had to be foolproof and easy to manipulate. No modern zip was used in case it became troublesome at the critical moment. Neither could small or delicate buttoning be used. The Mistress of the Robes, Mary, Duchess of Devonshire, whose duty it was to assist the Queen in donning this garment, would be wearing white kid gloves which might encumber the movements of her fingers.

Large buttons, few in number, but with equally large button-holes, were used. The Queen, firstly divested of her crimson robe by the Lord Great Chamberlain, would also take off her Diadem of

Precious Stones and the Collar of the Garter and would then put on this overdress and kneel at the crimson faldstool, bereft of all the world's vainglory.

I took the dresses in person and inadvisedly left by the front door in Bruton Street, accompanied by the stalwart Ted (Edward Dane), my van driver. To avoid attracting attention by using the house delivery van, or my own car, I hailed a taxicab. The large labelled box we were carrying was, however, inevitably noticed by passers-by. Soon there gathered around me a small crowd of onlookers that always, like magic, appear from nowhere.

I made a mental map of the route the taxicab would take. I said loudly, 'Oh, driver—would you take us to er—er—Victoria Station?'

'Sure, sir. Brighton or Continental?'

Three days later I was at the Savoy Hotel, supping as quietly as I could with some friends. Towards midnight the next morning's editions started to arrive, and I was delighted to see the pictured reproductions of the dress in all the newspapers. It was, I confess, a moment of magic for me as I walked away in the cool of the night, through the main streets of London, all a sight of colour and beauty.

I had decorated my house in vivid purple and white and the whole facade was brilliantly floodlit. Purple draperies were held up by gigantic court plumes in white enamelled metal, eight feet long. The crude scarlet of geraniums and golden fringes added a sharp note of contrast. At the windows of each floor were voluminous swags of curtain in white satin spotted with ermine tails. From the pavement level many passers-by had casually plucked those ermine tails, to keep, I imagine, as a souvenir of the contemporary London Coronation decoration. It was a nuisance each morning to replace those missing ermine tails.

It was past midnight and the street seemed deserted. I thought that I also would like to have one of my own ermine tails, actuated by a similar loyal and sentimental impulse. So I plucked one.

A voice from behind me said, 'Might I ask what you are doing?'

'Just plucking an ermine tail.'

'And by what right?' The speaker was wearing a smart raincoat.

'By the right of possession, and what has it got to do with you, anyway?'

'I am a detective. You'd better come with me to the station and answer on two charges: one, causing willful damage to property; two stealing.'

'Officer,' I said with all the dignity I could muster, 'I am Norman Hartnell.'

'Really? Well, that means nothing to me.'

'Oh, but you see I own this building, Inspector,' I replied patiently.

'And what proof have I that you are telling the truth?'

I pulled out my keys, inserted them in the locks and opened the front doors. The Inspector pointed a well-polished shoe, thrust one hand deep into the pocket of his raincoat and, with the other, thoughtfully fingered his clipped moustache.

'Good night,' he said quietly.

'Good night, Inspector.'

I went quickly up to bed, extremely relieved that I was not spending that night in gaol and anxious to snatch a few hours of sleep before the dawn of the great tomorrow.

— CHAPTER SIXTEEN —

Poetry and pageantry, they say, are England's greatest arts. In Westminster Abbey that day was shrined a moment of solemn history, the Coronation of Her Majesty Queen Elizabeth the Second. The clamour of colour in dress and uniform was already there, as I took my seat in the Queen's Box whither I had been ushered by Gold Staff Officers.

Immediately I ate a lump of sugar which I had secreted in the tail pocket of my black velvet Court suit and adjusted my buckled sword with its cut-steel hilt to a less uncomfortable angle, the better to concentrate upon the amazing scene spread before my wondering eyes.

I ate another lump of sugar. I was thankful to be early in getting to the Abbey to witness the arrival of all these noble men and women so gorgeously arrayed. Why didn't every one of them, every day, dress like this at breakfast time? What is the merit of choosing the drab when beauty hangs in the wardrobe?

I have never seen anything so transcendentally beautiful in my life. One after another the peeresses glide up the bright blue carpet, trailing their robes of crimson velvet, and hasten to their allotted seats like rubies in a hurry. Opposite are row upon row of peeresses mounting towards the very roof. They look like a lovely hunk of fruit cake; the damson jam of the velvet, bordered with the clotted cream of ermine and sprinkled with the sugar of diamonds. On my left are the peers, attired in their masculine version of ermine and velvet, their jam puff coronets nestling in their laps.

Lady Churchill arrives, silver-haired and lovely in a flowing dress of lavender chiffon, and talks gaily to people around her. The whole gathering seems like a wonderful party given by mistake in the early morning, and it surprises me that later, during the ceremony, hardly anyone adopts the attitude of prayer; for many, their dress makes it impossible.

The waving violins play celestial music and the voices of the choir trill, ring and rise like skylarks to the high vaulted roof of the sombre Abbey, once again alive with the colour of scarlet and gold and waving plumes. The doors are solemnly closed at 8.30am and the Processions begin.

Firstly come the members of the Royal Family. The beautiful women include the Countess of Harewood, the Marchioness of Carisbrooke and the Countess Mountbatten of Burma, followed by the Procession of the Royal and other Representatives of Foreign States. It is as though a jewel box has become unloosed and the precious jewels of myriad colours spill upon the velvet floor. A slender princeling wears a high-necked tunic of lemonade tinsel slashed with orange and a dog collar of emeralds and diamonds. His turban is of fine tangerine silk, exquisitely draped and clasped by rubies. An Eastern Imperial Highness gleams in silver and violet tissue, with strange feathers curling from a headgear of purple and amethyst. Peacock glory for another Prince, with brocade of lapis and malachite and ornaments of sapphire and emerald. A handsome potentate with the face of an oval chocolate has chosen creamy white, corded with gold, while a hero from Ruritania, moving elegantly to the gentle tintinnabulation of golden spurs, is encased in white cloth tunic and crimson breeches.

We see the rulers of States under the Queen's protection, headed by Her Majesty Queen Salote of Tonga. She wears a mantle of strawberry satin with what looks like a black knitting needle standing erect upon her darkly gleaming head. She walks gracefully upon sensible sandals of beige suede.

Then follow Their Royal Highnesses the Princes and Princesses of the Blood Royal. The Princess Royal in silver, looking strangely like her beloved mother, the late Queen Mary, followed by the Duchess of Gloucester, delightful in white satin.

The first of my own dresses to appear, apart from those of the peeresses, is beautifully worn by Her Royal Highness the Duchess of Kent, tall and classically beautiful as a Greek column in white satin and gold embroideries, with her daughter, the young Princess Alexandra of Kent, drifting in white tulle and lace glinting with golden thread.

A shaft of silvery sunlight suddenly pierces the lofty stained glass windows and splashes a pool of light upon the carpets of blue and gold. Her Royal Highness Princess Margaret now approaches, surrounded by six multi-coloured mediaeval Heralds of Somerset, Windsor, Richmond, York, Chester and Lancaster. Her gaze steadily fixed upon the High Altar, she moves in white beauty like a snow-drop adrift from its stem.

A wave of emotion passes over us as, in the next Procession, comes Her Majesty Queen Elizabeth The Queen Mother. We sense what poignant memories must now be hers, recalling a like occasion when she came to be crowned Queen to the Kingship of a beloved husband. The vivid blue riband of the Order of the Garter crosses the corsage of her white and golden gown, and the diamonds blaze with every measured step of her regal progress. She moves on to join the other members of her family in the Royal Gallery, just below where I stand.

There are high officers of State; Field Marshals; Admirals; officers of the Gentlemen-at-arms; then Heralds and Pages, some in scarlet or mustard or palest blue, according to the liveries of their masters.

I fumble nervously for another lump of sugar. My hand is trembling, for soon I shall be seeing the dress I had made, worn by Her Majesty the Queen for her Crowning. My mind wanders back to that day, almost exactly thirty years ago, when I resolved to establish myself in London. And I think suddenly of A. C. Benson, the Master of Magdalene College, and the number of Magdalene men who now surround the Queen. Her Majesty's Equerry, Lord Plunket; her Secretary of State for Air, Lord De L'Isle and Dudley; her secretary, Sir Michael Adeane and her Librarian at Windsor Castle, Sir Owen Morshead. All men of my old College …

I think of the Duchess of Gloucester and all that I owe to her. I think of the Queen Mother and her constant courtesy and kindliness. I think of the late King acting long ago as my guide to the art treasures of Buckingham Palace. I think of Queen Mary and my recent visit to see her gracefully carved effigy in St George's Chapel at Windsor Castle.

Just before Her Majesty's Procession, arrives His Royal Highness the Duke of Edinburgh, a dominant and romantic figure wearing the uniform of Admiral of the Fleet beneath his ermine and crimson velvet robe.

And then my eyes turn towards Her Majesty, for the Queen's Procession is approaching.

A clashing carillon of bells rings out over London; the great Firework music of Handel soars majestically to the rafters and the sweet voices of the choir become a paean of thanksgiving. The Abbey is filled with glorious and tremendous sound and the trumpets thunder in brassy triumph.

The Queen is come before our misty eyes. A slight and gentle figure, graceful in her glistening gown, her hands clasped and her eyes cast down. In beauty and solemnity, most slowly, she advances to her great and lonely station.

With those here in the great Abbey and the millions outside I join in a simple prayer. God save the Queen and long may she reign—for I feel that the whole world needs her.

INDEX